ONCE A PONZI TIME

This is a work of fiction. All of the characters, events, and organizations portrayed in this work are either products of the authors' imagination or used fictitiously.

Once A Ponzi Time
Copyright © 2013 by Joe Foust

All rights reserved. No part of this book may be reproduced in any form by any electronic or mechanical means including photocopying, recording, or information storage and retrieval without permission in writing from the author.

ISBN-13: 978-0692371244
ISBN-10: 0692371249

Cover Art by Jay Fosgitt
www.jayfosgitt.com

For information about production rights, visit www.onceaponzitime.com or write to joefoust@hotmail.com

Published by Sordelet Ink

Once A Ponzi Time

A Farce by
Joe Foust

Published by
Sordelet Ink

ONCE A PONZI TIME received its world premiere on July 3, 2013 at the Peninsula Players. It was directed by Linda Fortunato. Set Design by Sarah E. Ross, Lighting Design by Steve White, Sound Design by Josh Horvath, Costume Design by Samantha Jones, Prop Design by Sarah Ross. The Production Manager was Sarah Burnham. The Stage Manager was Deya S. Friedman. The Artistic Director was Greg Vinkler.

The play was written as a showcase for 5 actors, but other productions have used more. The orginal cast was as follows:

GRAMPS/DICK WELLINGTON: Neil Friedman
JUDITH/NATASHA/O'DONNELL: Molly Glynn
ED/SLADEMENGTON/SERGEY: Tim Monison
LOUIE: Noah Simon
HAROLD: Paul Slade Smith

THERE IS ONE INTERMISSION

Cast of Characters

Actor 1 - Harold
Actor 2 - Louie
Actor 3 - Gramps/Mr. Winkles/Dick Wellington
Actor 4 - Judith/Natasha/O'Donnell
Actor 5 - Ed Thompson/Agent Virginia Slademengton/Sergey

Setting

Living room of the Vanderdoff home

DEDICATED TO THE MEMORY OF
MY WIFE'S LAUGHTER

**Molly Glynn
1968-2014**

ACT I

SCENE I

(Curtain up on the Vanderdoff's Living Room. It is furnished with wealth and taste, but certainly cluttered. There is a front door that leads to the porch up right, a stairway down stage left leading up stairs, with a basement door under the stairs. There is a couch close to the upstage wall, with a window behind it; a coffee table in front of the couch; a bar down right; a desk stage left; a door up left that leads to the rest of the house; a swinging kitchen door mid-left; a television facing up stage, so the screen is not seen by the audience or perhaps it is on the fourth wall; chairs. As this is a very wet show, carpet is recommended)

(At the top of the show, we find GRAMPS sitting with his ventriloquist dummy, MR. WINKLES, on his knee. He is quietly practicing his art. GRAMPS lifts one of MR. WINKLES' legs and makes a fart sound. He lifts the other leg and makes a different fart sound. He is unsatisfied)

GRAMPS
That's hard to do without moving your lips.

(The front door opens and in steps HAROLD VANDERDOFF with his carry-on luggage)

HAROLD
Honey, I'm home! Hello dad.

(HAROLD kisses GRAMPS on top of his head. GRAMPS is startled because he didn't hear HAROLD come in)

GRAMPS
What the "H", "E", double hockey sticks! Don't sneak up on a fella!

HAROLD
Not wearing your hearing aids again?

GRAMPS
WHAT?!

(Enter JUDITH VANDERDOFF, HAROLD's wife)

JUDITH
Darling? You were supposed to call me when you landed.

HAROLD
My phone is completely dead from the long flight.

JUDITH
Well, since you're in one piece, I forgive you. *(She kisses him)* I missed you.

HAROLD
Not as much as I missed you.

JUDITH
How'd the trip go?

HAROLD
Capital! Count Von Umluat is keen to invest with Vanderdoff Investments.

JUDITH
That's wonderful news! I'm so proud of you. You are a financial genius.

HAROLD
Do you really think so?

JUDITH
Yes! You're a genius!

HAROLD
Oh, I wouldn't say that.

GRAMPS
Yes you would. I've heard you.

HAROLD
Have you ever heard of "selective hearing"?

GRAMPS
WHAT?!

JUDITH
Oh, Gramps.

HAROLD
How did Louie's meeting with the Havershards go?

JUDITH
Louie said it went swimmingly, they also want to invest.

HAROLD
Excellent, that's already more than enough.

JUDITH
More than enough what, dear?

HAROLD
Oh, nothing, nevermind.

JUDITH
I am in such a rush, I've got to go finish putting my face on - I wanted to make everything so nice for you when you got home and it's not.

HAROLD
As long as my beautiful wife is here, the place is perfect.

JUDITH
You charmer. I'm going to keep getting ready, so relax. I made coffee.

HAROLD
Thanks honey, but I've got to get to the office soon.

JUDITH
But you just got home.

HAROLD
Duty calls.

GRAMPS
You said "doodie".

HAROLD
Selective hearing.

GRAMPS
What?

JUDITH
Alright, but the next trip, I go with. I feel like I never see you.

HAROLD
Deal. *(She kisses him and exits. The desk phone rings and HAROLD answers it)* Hello? Oh, good morning Louie. I hear things went well with the Havershards. Really? When? That's unfortunate. But not devastating. I sealed the deal with Count Von Umluat, so at least we have one new big investor. Because new investors are key to our success. And today, I'll be making the most important investment in our history. I'll tell you all about it, come on by and we'll share a cab to the office. No, I left my car at work. That would be delightful, see you soon. *(HAROLD hangs up and quickly checks some paperwork)* Ok, minor setback, let's see: few months back rent, the Donnerby investment, carry the one... should be just enough. No reason to panic. *(Phone rings, he answers it)* Hello? *(He panics)* WHAT!? That's impossible! But there are sufficient funds! I know what I said, but please don't lock me out of the office. Look, let me make one quick call and I'll get right back to you. Charlie, don't change the locks, just wait, please? Fine I'll call you right back. *(Hangs up and makes another call)* No, no, no, this better not- Hello, Dave? It's Harold. Can you see if Count Von Umluat's deposit has cleared in my account? How do you know without checking? They froze his assets? Why? Oh, I see. When's the trial? Fine, thank you, yes, thank you. *(HAROLD hangs up, makes frustrated sounds and gestures)*

GRAMPS
Harold, is something wrong?

HAROLD
(Attempts to pull himself together quickly) No, why would you say that? *(He rushes to the phone and calls his office landlord back)* Hello, Charlie? Wait, listen, At least give me the new security code for the parking garage. *(Beat)* So I can get my car. *(Beat)* SO I CAN DRIVE TO THE BANK AND SORT THIS OUT! *(Beat)* Sorry, yes that was loud, I agree. Thank you. Wait, let me write this down. *(HAROLD searches for a pen)* Who keeps taking all my pens! *(GRAMPS clears his throat, clicks his pen and makes some notes. HAROLD to phone)* Hold on. Sorry. *(To GRAMPS)* Dad! Give me that pen! *(No reaction)* THE PEN! *(Nothing)* Dad! Would you please put in your hearing aids?

GRAMPS
What?

HAROLD
WOULD YOU PLEASE PUT IN YOUR HEARING AIDS?!

GRAMPS
Hand grenades?

(HAROLD gives up on GRAMPS and goes back to his ridiculous contortions to reach the pen)

GRAMPS
Oh I get it! Charades!

HAROLD
(Into phone) Thank you so much for your patience...

GRAMPS
(Guessing by HAROLD's contortions) It's a movie!

HAROLD
Pipe down! *(Into phone)* No, not you.

GRAMPS
Ooo! That Steve Martin movie... *(Yelling near phone)* YOU JERK!

HAROLD
No, no, no – you're not a jerk. I...

GRAMPS
(Yelling near phone) Psycho! Dirty Rotten Scoundrels! Bicycle Thief!

HAROLD
No, I know you didn't steal my bicycle, I... Hello?... Hello?

GRAMPS
Was it some kind of vegetable?

HAROLD
No, but you are.

GRAMPS
WHAT?!

HAROLD
Nevermind.

(Enter JUDITH)

JUDITH
Oh, darling, I almost forgot. Ed Thompson said he'd stop by this morning to talk about his investment.*(Handing him slips of paper)* You have several messages from a woman at the S.E.C.,

and O'Donnell left you a very angry message. I couldn't understand it all.

HAROLD
(Under his breath) yikes. *(To JUDITH)* Yes, yes, I'll take care of it.

JUDITH
When O'Donnell gets angry, I just think it's adorable. Don't you love Irish accents? *(She demonstrates her complete lack of skill with an Irish accent)* Arg, don't you go stealin' me pot o' gold now, ya ole potatah.

HAROLD
Indeed. Honey, it looks like I'll have to work from the home office again.

JUDITH
What? Why? I was going to have high tea here for the Frisbees for Guatemala Foundation.

HAROLD
I know, I'm sorry. I forgot I'm having the office painted today. Couldn't you have high tea at the club?

JUDITH
(Agreeably) Well, I suppose I could-

GRAMPS
Hey, Judith, look! I made Mr. Winkles some vampire teeth! *(Puts them in his dummy's mouth)*

MR. WINKLES
I vant to suck your sawdust!

JUDITH
Oh, that's very cute.

HAROLD
You know most ventriloquists try NOT to move their lips.

GRAMPS
What?

HAROLD
I don't know why he's suddenly taken up ventriloquism.

JUDITH
Sometimes people at his age just want some control. At least Mr. Winkles always says what Gramps wants to hear.

HAROLD
I just wish we could get him to meet some people. Join a club or something.

JUDITH
Maybe there's a ventriloquist club. I'll look into it. Now, I'm off to the charity bruncheon for the Society for the Ethical Treatment of Animals with One Eye. I do wish you'd reconsider co-chairing with me again. It was so much more fun with you around.

HAROLD
I know Darling, it was, and I wish I could, but -

JUDITH
You know, I could always cancel and be your sexy secretary for the day. *(Indicating the home office)* Try to help -

HAROLD
(A little too firmly) No! *(Tone change)* I mean, you would be far too distracting. I have to work.

JUDITH
Really, Harold, is money everything? I just want to spend some time together.

HAROLD
Judith, I swear to you, after today, one way or another everything is going to be very different.

JUDITH
Okay. I'll get out of your hair then. *(She kisses his cheek)* But do me a favor, and try not to make a habit of turning my home into your office. *(Pinches his cheek)*

HAROLD
No, of course not. As soon as I have the office fumigated, things will be back to normal.

JUDITH
I thought you said you were having it painted?

HAROLD
I am. So I certainly don't want bugs all over the fresh paint, do I?

JUDITH
Wha…?

HAROLD
(Scooting her towards the door) Oh, darling, you really should get going. Those animals with one eye aren't looking out for themselves, you know. *(Snatching up a piece of paper)* Speaking of which, I found a family to adopt little Pirate.

JUDITH
Really? That's wonderful! She's such a sweet kitty.

HAROLD
Mr. Pinkerton's daughter saw the poster I put up at the office, and fell in love with her big, beautiful, blue eye. *(HAROLD hands JUDITH the paper)* Here's their phone number.

JUDITH
You're a good man, Harold. *(Calling back to GRAMPS)* Bye Gramps!

GRAMPS
(Cupping his hand to his ear) What?

JUDITH
(Kindly) You know, we didn't buy you those hearing aids to decorate your bedside table. Harold?

HAROLD
Yes?

JUDITH
I love you.

HAROLD
I love you more.

JUDITH
Ha! Impossible!

(JUDITH exits. Door slam)

GRAMPS
HEY! Harold, you wanna hear some of my new material?

HAROLD
Oh, dad, I'm afraid I don't have time right now. *(He runs to the desk and desperately looks through paperwork)*

GRAMPS
Okay, here goes. *(He jumps up to do his ventriloquist routine)* Say hi to the people, Mr. Winkles.

MR. WINKLES
Hi to the people Mr. Winkles.

GRAMPS
(Mildly chastising him) Oh, now, Mr. Winkles.

MR. WINKLES
Just funnin' ya. Say! Here's a question: What is the last thing you wanna hear after giving Willie Nelson a sponge bath?

GRAMPS
What?

MR. WINKLES
I'm not Willie Nelson.

GRAMPS
(To HAROLD, looking for praise) Huh?

HAROLD
I don't get it.

GRAMPS
(Cupping his hand to his ear) What?

HAROLD
I said, I DON'T GET IT!

GRAMPS
Oh for the sake of Pete, come on. I mean you just gave Willie Nelson a sponge bath, right? Probably the only reason you agreed to it was because it was Willie Nelson.

(Phone rings, HAROLD answers it)

HAROLD
(To GRAMPS) Hold on... *(Into phone)* Yes?

GRAMPS
And now it's not Willie Nelson? I mean who have you been scrubbing for the last 40 minutes?

HAROLD
Sh!... *(Into phone)* Sorry. Come again? Yes, this is Harold Vanderdoff - And you are? Agent Virginia Salad-mening-ton? Yes, sorry, I'm terrible with names. Of the U.S. Securities and Exchange Commission? Good morning, ma'am, how are – oh yes, I see. Straight to business, of course. Prison? No, no, no, I see no need to involve the F.B.I. ...yes ma'am... I'm having the office paintigated. Oh, you have the home address? Well, today is not really... Already on your way? Ok, then; goodbye. *(HAROLD hangs up and slumps into a chair, utterly defeated)*

GRAMPS
Well, Mr. Picklepuss, somebody is down in the dumps. You know what might turn that frown upsidedown? The human ventriloquist routine! *(GRAMPS produces the mouth piece that is used for this routine)*

HAROLD
No!

GRAMPS
Oh, come on. *(As he is putting the mouth piece on himself)* You don't have to say or even do anything. I do all the talking for you. *(He turns to reveal himself with the mouth piece in, then demonstrates he can make the mouth move)* See? It's remote control! And it's fun. Look how much fun I'm

having. *(Arms akimbo on his hips like Superman)* Ha! Ha! Ha! Ha! Ha!

HAROLD
I shall never don that ridiculous device of yours, so please put it from your mind.

GRAMPS
But it's Fu-un!

(LOUIE enters through the front door)

LOUIE
Kno-ock! Morning Gramps!

GRAMPS
Louie! *(GRAMPS and LOUIE give each other an elaborate, secret club handshake)*

LOUIE
I see you're still working on the human ventriloquist routine.

GRAMPS
I am, but Harold won't play! He's no fun anymore.

HAROLD
Yes, yes, I'm quite the wet blanket.

GRAMPS
Remember when he used to be fun?

LOUIE
I'll do it again-

GRAMPS
No, it has to be Harold-

HAROLD
NO! Now shoo!

GRAMPS
Shooing me? Really? That's strike one, Harold. *(GRAMPS makes a frustrated sound and shuffles off)*

LOUIE
Morning Uncle Harold! Welcome back. Should we grab a cab?

HAROLD
No, Louie, looks like we'll be working from home again. I'm having the office painted.

LOUIE
Okalay-Dokalay! I brought us some get up and go juice, yes indeedy, abso-ma-tootly. Your favorite: half-caf-half-decaf, double foam cappuccino with four stevia leaf packets! That'll put some lead in your pencil, pardon my French. Now, I know you are the financial genius around here, and you have the investment portfolio well sorted out, but *(pointing to his head)* this little noodle had a thought. Why not *(playing the rhyme)* die.Versi-fie with a very small investment to hedge your bets? Could be just the thing, and I have a very exciting opportunity, Uncle Harold. Promise to hear me out?

HAROLD
Not in the least.

LOUIE
(Without missing a beat) Then I'll be quick. *(Beat)* Two words: Panda Fest.

HAROLD
Not this again.

LOUIE
Have you ever been to Panda Fest?

HAROLD
No.

LOUIE
They have it every year. Well, I have it every year, it's in my yard.

HAROLD
I see.

LOUIE
And I was trying to come up with this year's theme, and we've been thinking "It's Pandastic!" or "It's Pandacular!", but we ended up going with "It's Beary, Beary Fun! Spelled B-E-A-R-Y. But those darn silk screeners: the shirts came back and they said "It's fairy, fairy bun!" It was a complete clusterwhoops. Gosh, I musta wore my shirt for a week before I worked up the nerve to call and complain. But anyhoo, that silk screener used some language that wasn't fit for polite company, which made me awful nervous, but I told him to drink a tall glass of please-don't-be-so-rude and he hung up! So the long and the short of it is –

HAROLD
Stick to the short of it.

LOUIE
I need 600 dollars for new T-shirts.

HAROLD
Louie...

LOUIE
Now I know you're always telling me I have trou-

ble standing up for myself –

HAROLD
Sit down.

LOUIE
Okay. *(He sits)*

HAROLD
Now Louie, this is very important. You say the Havershards fell through, do you have any new investment leads?

LOUIE
No.

HAROLD
Are you sure?

LOUIE
Yes. I scraped the bottom of the proverbial barrel last week.

HAROLD
(Mumbling to himself, while walking to the downstage bar) I can fix this, I can fix this… *(Pours himself a drink. To LOUIE)* Would you like a drink?

LOUIE
It's not even 10 AM yet!

HAROLD
I like to get an early start on things. *(Offering some)* Peanuts?

LOUIE
No, thank you. Uncle Harold, what's wrong?

HAROLD
Oh Louie, I don't quite know how to tell you this. Vanderdoff Investments is in some trouble.

LOUIE
What kind of trouble?

HAROLD
Well, you know our quarterly interest payments are due today.

LOUIE
Yes, and you've done remarkably well again. Another 20% gain, abso-ma-tootly.

HAROLD
Yes, well, I'm afraid those figures may have been a little inflated.

LOUIE
How inflated?

HAROLD
Completely.

LOUIE
You mean no gains this quarter?

HAROLD
Right.

LOUIE
Well, yes, that's bad, but not terrible. That's what your split-strike conversion is ready to hedge against. At least there're no losses.

HAROLD
Well…

LOUIE
I mean for over a decade, you've been able to guarantee investors an average of 20% gain. One quarter of no gains, yet no losses, is still remarkable.

HAROLD
It would be, wouldn't it?

LOUIE
You've paid out hundreds of thousands of dollars to our friends over the years.

HAROLD
Not exactly.

LOUIE
Oh, come on, you're not making any sense.

HAROLD
I wasn't exactly paying interest on investments.

LOUIE
Well, where was the money coming from? Clearly, there were substantial profits.

HAROLD
Not so much profits earned, but money paid by subsequent investors, which was, believe you me, very earned. That was hard work!

LOUIE
But what about the split-strike conversion?

HAROLD
I was neither splitting nor striking.

LOUIE
What were you doing?

HAROLD
Sitting. Sitting very still on top of a large pile of money.

LOUIE
So, you're saying you weren't making any interest?

HAROLD
That's right.

LOUIE
But you were paying out supposed interest from new investor's stakes?

HAROLD
For the last several years, correct!

LOUIE
That's silly. That's something a silly person would say. The only way that would be possible *(Laughing at the very idea)* was if Vanderdoff Investments was merely a giant Ponzi scheme! Ha! Ha! Ha!

HAROLD
Yes.

LOUIE
(In denial) No.

HAROLD
Yes.

LOUIE
(Stronger denial) No.

HAROLD
Yes.

LOUIE
(Near tears) Yes?

(HAROLD nods, 'Yes')

LOUIE
(Beat. Then accepting the terrible weight of the truth) No.

(Suddenly LOUIE jumps up and grabs a paper bag.

He freaks out around the room, noisily breathing in and out of the bag)

HAROLD
Now, now, let's not do this. *(Starts to prep a drink for LOUIE)* Stop it now, this is childish.

(When next LOUIE fills the bag, HAROLD pops it. LOUIE shrieks in surprise. HAROLD hands him the drink. LOUIE downs it in one)

LOUIE
There was 18 million dollars in there, are you saying it's gone?

HAROLD
Gone, yes.

LOUIE
18 million?

HAROLD
All 18.

LOUIE
I had all my inheritance in there! All my savings!

HAROLD
Yes.

LOUIE
So you were just lining your pockets while throwing away your investor's money?

HAROLD
NO! I don't have two nickels to rub together. I never lined my pockets.

LOUIE
And you call yourself a criminal mastermind?

HAROLD
I don't! I'm not! I truly wanted to help those investors!

LOUIE
The investors! I can't believe I helped you find so many!

HAROLD
You're very good at it.

LOUIE
I thought you cared about them!

HAROLD
I do, deeply!

LOUIE
No wonder you made them sign those confidentiality agreements! You couldn't let anyone know!

HAROLD
No, but soon, everyone might know. An S.E.C. agent is on her way here, right now.

LOUIE
Securities and Exchange Commission?

HAROLD
Yes. *(LOUIE shrieks)* And it's the end of the financial quarter, so people will be here today demanding their interest payments. There's still a chance I can solve this once and for all. If not, this whole thing is coming down like a house of cards. Louie, I don't want you to get in any trouble. You just provided start up money. You didn't know about any of this.

LOUIE
Until you told me about it. Wait, why did you tell me about it? Now I'm culpable!

HAROLD
I know. If I can't solve this by 5:00 pm, I need you to turn me in.

LOUIE
Turn you in?

HAROLD
You won't be charged as an accessory.

LOUIE
You mean like a purse?

(Beat)

HAROLD
(Deadpan) No. Not like a purse. I mean like someone involved. You'll be completely in the clear. You might even get a reward.

LOUIE
(Innocent) I don't want to turn you in! I don't want to visit you in jail. Hear stories about your terrible lonesomeness. With no one to love or hold you. Sleeping cold and alone at night. With nothing but a threadbare blanket to keep you warm, missing the healing magic of human touch...

HAROLD
You're sweet. I mean that. But listen, you need to turn me in. And you have to promise me that you'll take care of Judith.

LOUIE
What?

HAROLD
This is going to kill her. You have to make sure she's all right. Do you understand? She's everything to me. You have to take care of her.

LOUIE
Wait, wait, wait, how could this even happen? When I gave you all my inheritance money, did you know you were just going to start a Ponzi scheme?

HAROLD
No! I wish I had never started any of this!

LOUIE
Then what happened?

HAROLD
The first three years we did alright. Better than alright. We actually made 20% interest almost every single quarter. The investors were thrilled. Word got around, others became interested, but...

LOUIE
But what?

HAROLD
Truth be told, the fund didn't do as well the next year. And the fifth? Even worse. But everyone was so impressed. I was helping people and they were so happy. We changed so many lives, Louie. And Judith was so proud! I couldn't let it end. So I started to fudge some results. Change some numbers. Those first three years had made me sure, sure I could catch up soon. Find the next big thing. But I couldn't. The only way to hang on was to find ways to pay the interest I was claiming to earn. I wish to God I could get

out of this mess! The irony is, after staying away from real investments for so long, I've stumbled onto an opportunity that can pay 2000% interest.

LOUIE
That is ironic.

HAROLD
What makes it even more ironic is that now I don't even have an office to work out of.

LOUIE
Technically speaking, that's not irony.

HAROLD
Excellent. Perhaps you could turn me in to the grammar police as well.

LOUIE
No, I think the grammar police would be more concerned with the structure of language or syntax rather than the misuse of a specific - *(HAROLD casually flings a throw pillow at LOUIE's head)* Ow!

HAROLD
Sometimes I wonder why I don't fire you.

LOUIE
Because I own 51% of the company?

HAROLD
That's the main reason.

LOUIE
Fair enough. Ok, now back it up. 2000%? That can't be right. What is this investment?

HAROLD
Remember Wayne Rosner? That guy I got to adopt that docksu- dashsh- that wiener dog?

LOUIE
You mean Cyclops?

HAROLD
Exactly. Well, he told me about it. *(Holding up a file)* It's called the Donnerby investment. The numbers look good. I finished my due diligence report and even had a quantitative analyst take a look at it, and now he's investing his own money.

(LOUIE holds out his hand for the file, but HAROLD, pointedly puts it in his desk drawer)

LOUIE
Okay, how much would we need to invest to recoup lost funds? Let's see... 2000% at... *(scribbling on a pad)*... carry the one...

HAROLD and LOUIE
900,000 dollars –

HAROLD
– I know, would put us back at the 18 mil mark, enough to pay everyone back and walk away, Shut the doors on Vanderdoff Investments for good, so I can spend the rest of my life trying to make it up to Judith. But we have no new prospects for investors and I've spent every dime I had paying out "so-called" interest.

LOUIE
Wait, you mean you spent all your own money trying to help people out of this?

HAROLD
Yes!

LOUIE
That's kinda sweet.

HAROLD
Louie, listen: the Donnerby investment needs to be made by three o'clock today. I'm going to do my best to make it happen. If not, I need you to turn me in.

LOUIE
But what if I don't?

HAROLD
Then we might be cell mates and I'd let you have top bunk. But I promised your father I would keep you out of trouble.

LOUIE
No, I mean what if I don't need to turn you in?

HAROLD
I don't follow.

LOUIE
When my dad passed away, you took care of me. You've been like a father to me, Uncle Harold. And I think it's time I step up to the plate and take care of you. What if we found the money for the Donnerby investment?

HAROLD
But how?

LOUIE
I know we can do this. We can figure it out. Don't forget what I always hear you say: That you are brilliant!

HAROLD
Well, I am, but –

LOUIE
Guess what? Turns out the nephew doesn't fall

too far from the tree.

HAROLD
What?

LOUIE
And I have a plan.

HAROLD
You thought of a new lead?

LOUIE
Nope. Better. A plan.

HAROLD
A plan?

LOUIE
A plan. We just have to get a little less than a million dollars together before three o'clock. How fast will you see the return?

HAROLD
Almost immediately. Before the end of the business day.

LOUIE
Excellent! That makes our job all the easier. Uncle Harold, you believed in me when almost no one else would. You helped me up when I fell down. You gave me hope at the darkest times of my life, and now, by golly, I'm gonna do the same for you. I just know we will sail through this thing, smooth as butter, and cross the finish line, smelling like roses!

HAROLD
Toss in a few more mixed metaphors and we'll have a salad.

LOUIE
Don't make fun. I love you Uncle Harold. We're gonna get through this thing side-by-side. A team! You and me. And I know you're worried, but worry no longer, for I have a plan.

HAROLD
(Hopes rising) Okay, what is it?

LOUIE
My plan?

HAROLD
Yes!

LOUIE
(Dramatic pause as LOUIE nods his head, knowingly. He lifts an arm and speaks facing out) The universe provides.

(Pause)

HAROLD
And?

LOUIE
And what?

HAROLD
What's the plan?

LOUIE
That is the plan.

HAROLD
What's the plan?

LOUIE
(Goes back to the holding arm up position, checks in with HAROLD. Looks out) The universe provides.

(Pause)

HAROLD
(Calmly) The universe provides.

LOUIE
Ya-huh.

HAROLD
That's the plan?

LOUIE
(Confident he has saved the day) That's the plan!

(Pause)

HAROLD
(Explodes) How is that a plan?!

LOUIE
We sit back and wait for the universe to provide.

HAROLD
That is not a plan!

LOUIE
Sure it is.

HAROLD
Are you serious?! Perhaps I should sit back and wait for the universe to provide a very long fork so I can stick it in your eye!

LOUIE
Hey now.

HAROLD
I have never heard of anything so absolutely idiotic in all my days!

LOUIE
Now I think you need to drink a tall glass of

please-don't-be-so-rude. *(HAROLD stares at him, deadpan)* Oh, look... *(LOUIE bends over and picks up an imaginary object from the floor and holds it out for HAROLD)* you dropped a smile. *(Attempts to place the 'smile' on HAROLD's face)* Bing!

(HAROLD screams in frustration and takes off running after LOUIE, who scampers off. A chase ensues)

LOUIE
I don't have insurance!

(As LOUIE runs past the kitchen door, it suddenly flies open and splat goes HAROLD on the upstage side. Enter GRAMPS with a frying pan full of scrambled eggs. GRAMPS sits down and turns on the TV at full volume. The intro to The Lawrence Welk Show is heard. GRAMPS happily munches on the eggs he has brought from the kitchen. HAROLD rubs his head, while marching over to GRAMPS)

HAROLD
Dad, do you realize you just - ?

(HAROLD is blocking GRAMPS' view, so GRAMPS pushes him out of the way with his quadruped cane)

GRAMPS
I'm trying to watch my progrim! Lawrence Welk comes on at ten o'clock! At ten o'clock, I watch The Lawrence Welk Progrim!

(HAROLD picks up the remote and, from behind GRAMPS, turns the volume down to nothing. GRAMPS doesn't seem to notice, and keeps watching and munching)

GRAMPS
Bubbles!

(HAROLD tries spiking the volume up)

LOUIE
LOUD!

(HAROLD turns the volume down. Nothing from GRAMPS)

HAROLD
Why don't you go put in your hearing aids?

GRAMPS
What?

HAROLD
(Starts helping him to stand) Why don't you go put in your hearing aids?

GRAMPS
What am I doing?

HAROLD
You're going to put in your hearing aids!

GRAMPS
They're going to put on a Ham Parade? Why didn't you say so? I love ham! And parades! *(GRAMPS raises his finger in the air with a sudden idea)* I'll go get the lawn chairs! *(GRAMPS rushes, excitedly, toward the basement, then rushes back and quickly finishes his eggs, then runs off to the basement)*

LOUIE
No, Gramps, he meant –

HAROLD
(Turning off the TV) Oh, let him get his hopes up.

(Ding dong)

HAROLD
Who's that?

LOUIE
(Looking out window) It's Ed Thompson.

HAROLD
At least it's not the SEC.

LOUIE
How much interest is he owed?

HAROLD
Around 50,000.

LOUIE
Oh, dear, oh, dear, oh, dear...mmm.

HAROLD
Now, listen, Louie: I used to be a lot like you. I was terrified by situations like this. But I've learned over the years that the important thing is you must take initiative and seem to be in charge. Come on, Louie, buck up! Give me 2 seconds and let him in. *(to himself)* Oh, dear, oh, dear, oh, dear... mmmm.

(HAROLD rushes over to his desk and quickly tests his fake phone. NOTE: at the desk there is one fake ringing phone and one real phone that are clearly different, and used when appropriate. When necessary, HAROLD makes the false phone ring by using a foot pedal)

LOUIE
That phone was fake?

HAROLD
Yes

LOUIE
It always used to ring when I was telling you about Panda Fest –

HAROLD
Louie!

(HAROLD begins typing busily at his computer and nods to LOUIE to open the door. LOUIE opens the door and in steps ED THOMPSON, a mousy little man who looks like a walking apology)

LOUIE
Good morning, Mr. Thompson!

ED
Good morning, Louie. Good morning, Mr. Vanderdoff.

HAROLD
(Grunts, but continues 'working'. He answers a ringing phone) What? You tell the senator I'll call him back when I'm good and ready! *(He slams the phone down)*

(Enter GRAMPS from the basement wearing a straw boater with American flags in it, carrying lawn chairs, and a cooler)

GRAMPS
Come on! Let's get to the Ham Parade already! We're burning daylight here!

LOUIE
Oh, dear. Gramps, there isn't a Ham Parade.

GRAMPS
(Noticing ED) Who the heck are you?

ED
Ed Thompson, sir. Your wife used to be in my bridge club, God rest her soul. I remember her so fondly.

GRAMPS
Who'd she fondle?

LOUIE
No, Gramps. *(To ED)* He's not wearing his hearing aids.

GRAMPS
(Pointing at ED) He's taking us to the parade?

LOUIE
No, Gramps…

GRAMPS
(To ED) Listen, when they start throwing out the hams, grab as many as you can. *(Holding up cooler)* We'll put them in this!

LOUIE
(Grabbing GRAMPS, and speaking slowly and loudly to his face) GRAMPS! THERE IS NO HAM PARADE!

GRAMPS
(Turning on ED) And I suppose this is your fault, huh? Did you cancel it? I will slap the green apple out of your mouth, son!

LOUIE
(Again, slowly and loudly) GRAMPS! THERE NEVER WAS A HAM PARADE!

GRAMPS
Then why did you let me get my hopes up?

HAROLD
Well, I honestly thought you'd go down to the basement and forget why you were there.

GRAMPS
Strike two, son, strike two. Keep this up and you'll get yours.

HAROLD
You may be right.

GRAMPS
Oh, I know I am. Now if you'll excuse me, I have some sulking to do. *(GRAMPS starts to exit. Grabs Mr Winkles on the way out)* Come on.

MR WINKLES
Where we going? *(GRAMPS exits)*

LOUIE
Sorry about that.

ED
No, no, I'm sure it was my fault.

LOUIE
Or mine. *(HAROLD clears his throat)* Or not. What can we do ya for, Mr. Thompson?

ED
Well, just thought I'd pop by to check the old numbers.

LOUIE
Righty-ho! *(LOUIE turns to go get a folder from the desk, and HAROLD, still 'working' hard, flings it at LOUIE like a frisbee)* Oof. *(He shows*

the paperwork to ED)

ED
Oh, yes, another 20%. Well played, well played.

HAROLD
(Grunts and answers a phone) Buy! Buy at 90! *(Slams the phone down)*

LOUIE
Would you like a check for the interest or just roll it over into the next quarter?

ED
Well, I...

LOUIE
I know the checkbook is around here somewhere. *(Rummages around HAROLD's desk)* Uncle Harold, have you seen the –

HAROLD
(Taking whatever is in LOUIE's hands and slamming it back down on the desk) Not now!

ED
(To LOUIE) Oh, no, of course, just let it roll over then.

LOUIE
Okalay-dokalay, and we'll see you sometime at the office then. *(Ushering him towards the door)*

ED
(Breaking away from LOUIE) Actually, um, er... There is something else I wanted discuss with you Mr. Vanderdoff.

HAROLD
I'm rather busy here, Ed.

ED
Oh, yes, I know, I can see that, and I know your time is valuable, and I would certainly, in no way, shape, or form, want to waste it…

HAROLD
You're doing a pretty good job of it so far.

ED
Yes, yes, well I'll get straight to the point. I know I signed a confidentiality agreement, but…

HAROLD
Ed, I don't like the sound of this –

ED
Yes, no, I'm sorry… but I did a little something…

HAROLD
(Keeping a lid on it) What have you done?

ED
Last quarter I let someone invest under my name, I just bundled their money with mine.

HAROLD
What?

ED
You see, he's a very powerful man, and rather hard to say no to –

LOUIE
Oh, I know that feeling.

ED
And, anyway, I happened to let slip that I had this genius advisor, and he couldn't believe the numbers –

HAROLD
Go on.

ED
Yes, well, he wanted to invest with me as sort of a test –

HAROLD
A test? Like of my patience?

ED
Again, so sorry, but after these quarterly results, he's very anxious to meet you and he has a great deal of money to invest.

HAROLD
(Starting to bubble with excitement) A lot of money you say?

ED
Oh, yes. He's the wealthiest man I know.

HAROLD
Ha.

LOUIE
Squee!

HAROLD
Hee, hee.

LOUIE
Yep.

HAROLD
Well, that's...good. This calls for a toast!

ED
Oh, thank goodness, I was afraid you'd be upset with me.

HAROLD
Upset?

ED
Well, people always seem to be upset with me. If you don't mind me asking, why aren't you upset?

HAROLD
Well, let's just say you caught me on a good day. I've recently been considering taking on some new investors. Right, Louie?

LOUIE
That's right. This is great news.

HAROLD
(Going to the bar and opening a bottle of champagne from the ice bucket) Champagne all around!

ED
It's only 10:30 in the morning.

HAROLD
(Quickly adding orange juice) Mimosas all around! *(Begins passing out the glasses)*

LOUIE
(Singing to tune of Farmer In The Dell) Mimosas all around! Mimosas all around! Heigh-ho the Derry-Oh! Mimosas.... *(Stops as HAROLD stares)*

HAROLD
A toast! To good friends!

LOUIE
To good friends, old and new!

HAROLD
Here, here!

(They encourage ED to drink. He does. ED is clearly not a drinker. His eyes bulge, and he sputters and coughs. HAROLD begins hitting him on the back. This seems to make it worse)

LOUIE
Oh my stars! He's choking! What's good for choking?

HAROLD
Whiskey!

(HAROLD continues hitting ED on the back, thinking harder is sure to help, whilst LOUIE rushes to the bar and, not knowing any better, pours a very tall whiskey, then rushes back. HAROLD is concentrating on ED's back and doesn't notice the size of the pour)

LOUIE
Here, drink this!

(ED manages to drink it all down. A moment of calm. All may be well. HAROLD notices the large glass)

HAROLD
How much whiskey did you give him?

LOUIE
Just a glassful.

HAROLD
Wha-?

(Nope. Eye of the storm. ED sputters and reacts to the burning of the whiskey. He stumbles around the room. HAROLD follows and helps by pounding his back whenever he's still. LOUIE fans him with some silly object he has found. ED makes

ridiculous sounds. He finally passes out sitting up on the floor)

LOUIE
Sweet Georgia Peaches, what happened?

HAROLD
I don't know; might have to do with the entire glass of whiskey you gave him!

LOUIE
Was that too much?

HAROLD
No, apparently it was just right.

LOUIE
(Bending over ED) Well, now what do we do?

(ED wakes up with a hiccup. LOUIE is startled)

HAROLD
Are you alright.

ED
Feeling pretty good.

HAROLD
Listen, Ed, I'm so sorry.

ED
Sorry is my speciality.

HAROLD
Yes, now don't worry about that confidentiality agreement. You were just trying to help out a friend. You know how dearly I value friendship. And if you trust this friend of yours, I trust your judgment, old friend. Let's set up a meeting, and see if he's someone I feel I could work with.

ED
(Somewhat pie-eyed) OK, buddy.

HAROLD
What is your friend's name?

ED
Harold Vanderdoff, that's you buddy. My friend. *(ED playfully touches HAROLD's nose)* Boop!

HAROLD
Yes, yes. I am your friend. But whose money did you invest?

ED
(In his own world) Whose-money-whose-money-whose-money-who's money?-batter-swiiing!

(ED sits on the desk, crosses his legs, puts his elbow on his top knee, and rests his chin on his fist. He's feeling pretty good)

HAROLD
Ed! Who was your friend that invested the hundred thousand dollars?

(ED starts to snore. HAROLD kicks the foot of the crossed leg which makes a chain reaction as if ED punched himself in the chin)

ED
Five more minutes, mom.

HAROLD
(Grabbing him roughly) Ed! Who was the bundled investor?!

ED
Oh, Dick Wellington.

LOUIE
Dick Wellington? The Dick Wellington? As in Dick Wellington, C.E.O. of Wellington Worldwide Empire Industries?

ED
Yup. Well, actually, his wife.

HAROLD
Are you saying Natasha Wellington gave you the hundred thousand dollars to invest?

ED
(Shaking head 'no') Yes. *(Shaking head 'yes')* No. *(Making circles with his head)* Sorta. I tole her all about Vanderdoff Investments, how you saved me from being foreclosed, and she was re-all interested-did. *(Trying again)* Interesti-did. *(Again)* Interres- *(Gives up)* She wants her husband to invest. She tole him to gimme the money. Gimmie the money!

HAROLD
And now they want a meeting?

ED
Yepper-depper! Today! *(He touches HAROLD's nose again)* Boop. You know, my Aunt Myrtle liked me better than any of her other nephews. *(ED falls asleep again, with sudden snoring)*

HAROLD
We've got to sober him up and make this meeting happen today! Take him to the upstairs bathroom and get him to throw up.

LOUIE
How am I supposed to do that?

HAROLD
(Handing LOUIE a picture from his desk) Show him this picture of Gramps in his swim trunks.

LOUIE
Ugh! Why is that on your desk? —

HAROLD
And if that doesn't do the trick *(grabbing an ostrich feather from a decorative arrangement)*, shove this down his throat. Then get him to drink this. *(Hands LOUIE a half-full pot of coffee)* Dick Wellington. What a gold mine! I can't believe this just fell into our laps! Remember what I taught you. *(Holding arm up like LOUIE did)* The universe provides.

LOUIE
But, I —

HAROLD
You should listen to me with a more attentive ear if you want to better yourself. Now off you go!

(LOUIE struggles to carry ED, the picture, the feather and the pot of coffee up the stairs)

ED
These stairs are weird...

(They exit. HAROLD is very pleased with himself. He goes over to the stereo and puts on some music, mayhaps 'Celebrate' by Kool & the Gang. He begins to move a little to the music. This evolves to him prancing around the room to the music. He starts full on dancing. JUDITH enters and is gobsmacked. She watches HAROLD. He dances even more elaborately. Who knew he had it in him? He spins around, gives JUDITH a

thumbs up, spins back to out and continues dancing. Double take as he realizes JUDITH is here. He quickly turns off the music. Pause as he tries to hide his embarrassment and heavy breathing)

HAROLD
Hey. Hi. You're here. Back soon.

JUDITH
We had to adjourn the bruncheon early, because Mary Shmula got a bit tipsy and tried to give all the men hernia tests. She's the worst co-chair, but what on earth are you doing?

HAROLD
(Beat) Celebrating.

JUDITH
Celebrating what?

HAROLD
Vanderdoff Investments has a new big lead.

JUDITH
Well, that's wonderful news, darling. I'm glad to see you celebrating, all work and no play is- you know. So absolutely everyone at the bruncheon this morning was all atwitter about you. They are so excited about the quarterly payments coming out today. I am so proud of you, helping all our friends and more importantly, those less fortunate than ourselves. Now Mrs. Olson can afford that transplant surgery for her daughter.

HAROLD
Yes, I, erm…

JUDITH
Just look at the good you're doing!

HAROLD
Judith, I have a confession to make.

JUDITH
No, wait. I have a confession of my own. It has just been eating at me. You know how reluctant you were to let me place charity money into the Vanderdoff investment fund? Well, I know it was sneaky, but I bundled several of my charity's standing funds under the name "Francois Nom Duplume" and "Francois" invested through Louie. He never even knew it was me.

HAROLD
Oh, no. I wish you would have talked to me about that first

JUDITH
See! I knew it would make you uncomfortable. That's why I went behind your back. But look how smart I was! You've made every one of those charities thousands of dollars! I get to look like a big shot, all because of you. You really help people, Harold. It's all you've ever wanted to do. You make this world a better place. *(She kisses him)* Now, what was it you wanted to tell me, dear?

HAROLD
I'm... I'm just so happy.

JUDITH
Well so am I. *(Looks at her watch)* Oh dear, before the high tea, I've got to run to a fundraiser for Crutches on Wheels. You keep up the good work, Harold. I love you!

(exit JUDITH)

HAROLD
(All by himself) I love you too.

(Enter LOUIE. He notices HAROLD is off in his own world)

LOUIE
Uncle Harold?

HAROLD
Louie. How's Thompson coming along?

LOUIE
Much better I think. He's finishing the coffee.

(ED comes down the stairs, wiping his brow with a kerchief)

HAROLD
Feeling better?

ED
Man, that's good coffee. That coffee's good. What kind of coffee is that?

HAROLD
Ed?

ED
You know, I don't normally drink coffee.

HAROLD
Here. I'll take that.

(HAROLD takes the empty coffee pot and goes to put it back on the burner)

ED
So sorry about that. *(ED does a bit of shaking)*

HAROLD
Quite alright, quite alright. Now, what time to

you want to bring Dick Wellington by?

ED
Dick? Right, Dick! Of course Dick, and Natasha will want to be here as well. She'll insist on it. Shall we say three o'clock?

(HAROLD and LOUIE exchange a quick look)

HAROLD
I actually have an awfully busy afternoon lined up, but I could squeeze in a little time at lunch. Shall we say 12:30?

ED
12:30, 12:30, 12:30. Got it! I'll stop by and introduce you. And again, I am so sorry, so very sorry, I can't tell you how sorry I am.

HAROLD
(Ushering him to the front door) Then stop trying. We'll see you in a few hours then.

ED
Hey! Watch how fast I can run!

(ED runs off. HAROLD shuts the door)

LOUIE
See? Things are looking up. I have a good feeling about this.

(LOUIE leans over and flicks the stereo back on. He starts to dance to the music. HAROLD watches him, filled with worry and remorse. He sinks into a chair as LOUIE continues dancing. The lights fade)

END OF SCENE ONE

ACT I

SCENE II

(Lights up on HAROLD, alternating between bustling about making sure things are 'just so' for DICK WELLINGTON's arrival, and going over some paperwork. LOUIE is at the computer and GRAMPS is next to him, trying out his new material)

GRAMPS
Alright, alright, how bout this one?

MR. WINKLES
Say, whaddaya call a nosey pepper?

GRAMPS
I dunno. What?

MR. WINKLES
Jalapeño business! *(MR. WINKLES bobs his head back and forth)*

GRAMPS
See, and then I give him some head sass.

(Beat as GRAMPS waits for LOUIE'S reaction)

LOUIE
I like the sass. But, I don't get it.

GRAMPS
Jalapeño business! Like "all up in yo' business?"

LOUIE
Oh, I see. It is funny, once you explain it.

GRAMPS
(GRAMPS makes a frustrated sound) Hey Harold, 'member earlier when you said you'd do the human ventriloquist routine with me?

HAROLD
That never happened.

GRAMPS
'Member?

HAROLD
I will never, ever do that! Do you even know me?

GRAMPS
(Mishearing HAROLD) Yes, you're annoying me!

HAROLD
Put in your hearing aids! Shoo! Shoo! We're busy!

GRAMPS
ARRGH! You're very close to strike three. *(He storms off)*

HAROLD
(To LOUIE) Well, what have you found out?

LOUIE
Ok, seems Dick Wellington has his fingers in all sorts of pies. Oil companies. Private military and

security contracting. Pharmaceuticals, you name it, Wellington Worldwide Empire Industries is knee-deep in it. I can't even conceive of how many billions he must be worth –

HAROLD
Yes, yes, we knew all that. What can you tell me about him?

LOUIE
What do you mean?

HAROLD
What makes him tick? What makes him angry? How does he relax? That kind of thing.

LOUIE
Oh, well, that's a bit harder. He seems pretty private. *(Typing away)* Let's see here. His third wife, Natasha, Russian, is 20 years younger than he is. Every year he goes on a baby seal clubbing safari. Wait, they have those? That's terrible.

HAROLD
Anything else?

LOUIE
(Looking at computer) Yikes. I wouldn't mention his hair. So what's the plan, Stan?

HAROLD
Well, playing hard ball seems the best plan of attack.

LOUIE
Oh dear, Oh dear, Oh dear, mmmmmmmmmmmmm.

HAROLD
Louie, you can't be so afraid of conflict.

LOUIE
Oh, yes I can!

HAROLD
Louie, I used to fear conflict, but I've learned that with a bully like Dick Wellington, you need to take initiative and appear a bigger bully.

(Ding dong)

HAROLD
Alright. Show time.

(HAROLD goes to the desk as LOUIE opens the door. Enter ED THOMPSON, DICK WELLINGTON, and his wife, NATASHA. The WELLINGTONS practically ooze wealth. He has a terrible Donald Trump hair piece. She's a dangerous kind of sexy)

LOUIE
Welcome to Vanderdoff Investments! I'll just get Mr. Vanderdoff. *(Crossing to HAROLD, who is pretending to be on the phone)* Mr. Vanderdoff –

HAROLD
(On phone) Stop bothering me will you? Can't you see I'm busy? *(Turning to see DICK WELLINGTON, still on phone)* Quit being such an insufferable- Dick ...Wellington! *(Into phone)* I'll call you back. *(Hangs up)* How are you?

DICK WELLINGTON
Alright, Vanderdoff, my time is valuable, so I'll give you five minutes to show me something that impresses me. *(Looks at watch)* Go!

HAROLD
Very well then. *(Points to the front door)* There is

the door. Impressive, isn't it? Feel free to use it. *(Returns to his 'work')*

DICK WELLINGTON
(After a moment of amazement) Look here, Vanderdoff, I didn't come all the way across town to be insulted by some two-bit investment advisor working out of his living room!

HAROLD
I beg to differ. It appears you did.

DICK WELLINGTON
How dare you!

HAROLD
Your sense of entitlement is wildly misplaced here, Mr. Wellington. I don't work for you. I neither need, nor did I solicit, your money. It was you who secretly piggybacked your money onto one of my client's investments, entirely without my knowledge, as some sort of undignified test of my financial prowess. I agreed to meet with you as a favor to my dear old friend, Ted Thompson here.

ED
Ed.

HAROLD
Yes, Ed. I have no intention of dancing like an organ grinder's monkey to earn your business.

DICK WELLINGTON
Do you know I could crush you like a –

NATASHA
(Cutting him off) Darling. *(To HAROLD)* Mr. Wanderdoff. I apologize for my husband's behav-

ior. He only barks this loudly when he's afraid the other dogs no longer think he's the alpha. It is I who wanted to test your skills. I wanted to make sure I wasn't wasting my husband's time before pushing him into a meeting. Please, it is me you must forgive.

HAROLD
Mrs. Wellington –

NATASHA
Natasha, please.

HAROLD
Natasha, I apologize. I have been known to bark quite loudly myself. Sometimes my temper gets the better of me. Mr. Wellington, would you like to have a conversation?

DICK WELLINGTON
I would. *(To ED)* Thompson, beat feet.

ED
Sir?

DICK WELLINGTON
Take a walk till your hat floats. We don't need you here anymore.

ED
Ah, yes, thank you, sir. *(Quickly heads to the door and opens it)* May I just say, Harold Vanderdoff is an excellent financial advisor. I've heard him say so on many occasions. (ED exits)

DICK WELLINGTON
And you. *(Pointing to NATASHA)* Remember, your only job is to stand there and look shiny. *(Being as respectful as he can manage to HAROLD)*

Act One, Scene Two

So, Mr. Vanderdoff, what's the game?

HAROLD
Well, I run a split-strike conversion fund of funds. I've consistently delivered an average of 20% interest returns for over a decade.

DICK WELLINGTON
So what's the skinny? Insider trading?

HAROLD
You know I can't say yes to that.

DICK WELLINGTON
Front running?

HAROLD
Possibly. Why all the questions, are you writing a book?

(DICK's phone rings)

DICK WELLINGTON
(To HAROLD) Wait! *(Into phone)* What? Fine, make it quick, I'm in a meeting. *(Points to LOUIE)* You. *(Back to phone)* Go. *(Back to LOUIE, and points at the bar)* Scotch!

LOUIE
Sir, I am not the butler –

DICK WELLINGTON
SCOTCH!

(LOUIE runs to pour him a scotch, neat)

DICK WELLINGTON
(Into phone) Contaminated infant formula? No, don't pull it, sell it in Mexico. Then why am I paying 100 lawyers every month? *(Back to LOUIE who has arrived with his scotch)* Soda *(LOUIE*

goes to put a splash of soda in the scotch. DICK goes back to phone) Next? Protesting what? Fine. Well, if everyone is so afraid of toxic waste being dumped so close to the convent, then throw the whole load behind the orphanage. Maybe those kids will mutate into something more adoptable. *(Finishes scotch. To LOUIE)* Again. *(Into phone)* Next. A personal day for what? Your wife's funeral? Listen, if you ever ask me for a personal day again, it'll be your funeral. Now get back to work! *(Hangs up. To HAROLD)* You were saying?

LOUIE
(Referring to DICK's futuristic phone) What is that thing?

DICK WELLINGTON
The iPhone 9.

LOUIE
There is no iPhone 9.

DICK WELLINGTON
Not that you know about. *(To HAROLD)* We were saying?

HAROLD
Right, a split-strike conversion –

DICK WELLINGTON
Oh, this crap again.

HAROLD
Alright, get out.

DICK WELLINGTON
What?

HAROLD
Beat feet. Take a walk till your hat floats.

(A beat. Everyone is amazed at HAROLD's chutzpah)

DICK WELLINGTON
(Laughs) Very well, Harold, I'm going to be frank with you. I rarely meet someone who has the juice to stand up to me, so I'll freely admit: you intrigue me. I don't really want to ask you a lot of questions about what you do, because I'm pretty sure there's something squirrelly going on, and I'd prefer a little plausible deniability.

LOUIE
(To HAROLD) Ah! See? *(Lamely covering)* Yes.

DICK WELLINGTON
(Pulling out his phone) So, here's the deal. Give me your account number and I'll transfer 500,000 dollars as my own little test —

HAROLD
A million.

DICK WELLINGTON
What?

HAROLD
I'm not interested unless it's at least a million.

DICK WELLINGTON
(Laughs) Okay, Mr. Big Britches, let's make it a cool million. *(LOUIE shows DICK the account number on a piece of paper as DICK works on his phone)* See what you can do with it in three months. But I warn you, I am absolutely not someone you want to disappoint. There, I've transferred the money to your account. *(Puts phone away. To NATASHA)* Happy?

NATASHA
Da.

DICK WELLINGTON
Good. Let's go. *(Starts to exit)*

NATASHA
Actually, I want to stay here.

DICK WELLINGTON
(Suspicious) Why?

NATASHA
Unlike you, I'm wery curious about a split-strike conwersion. I found this inwestment for you and I want to understand it fully.

DICK WELLINGTON
I bet you do. *(To HAROLD)* Don't touch my wife.

HAROLD
I beg your pardon?

DICK WELLINGTON
You heard me. *(To LOUIE)* That goes for you too, pipsqueak.

LOUIE
Wha...?

DICK WELLINGTON
Yes, yes, I'm sure it's not in your nature, but *(Referring to NATASHA)* when the church is this beautiful, you might be tempted to attend services once or twice. Don't. *(Handing her some money)* Here's cab fare.

NATASHA
This is barely enough.

DICK WELLINGTON
Then you should consider walking. You've been packing on some poundage these days. Remember, trophy wives are meant to be mounted, not stuffed. I'll see you later. *(He goes to kiss her, she turns her cheek to catch it. DICK points to his eyes then points to HAROLD and LOUIE. He exits)*

NATASHA
A real charmer, isn't he?

HAROLD
I really do apologize, Mrs. Wellington –

NATASHA
Natasha.

HAROLD
Natasha – but I really must get back to work. Is there something specific you'd like to know?

NATASHA
No, no, please, work. I'll just watch for a bit.

HAROLD
(This is awkward) Very well. *(HAROLD goes to his desk to 'work')*

LOUIE
So, Mrs. Wellington, I notice you're on the hunt for investments. Have you ever considered movie producing?

NATASHA
No.

LOUIE
(Producing a bound manuscript) Well, I've been working on a screenplay, it's a romantic comedy. Sort of a "panda meets girl, panda loses girl,

panda gets girl back" kind of thing. It's called "Tiny Pandancer". I've based the character names on the actors I want to secure for the roles. I think they'll be flattered. There's Pandy Patinkin, Pandra Bullock, and Apandalina Jolie. Feel free to give it a read.

NATASHA
I'll be sure to do that.

LOUIE
I'm hoping to premiere it at next year's Panda Fest, have you ever been to Panda Fest?

NATASHA
No.

LOUIE
They have it every year. Well, I have it every year, it's in my yard –

NATASHA
Louie, it is Louie, right?

LOUIE
Yes ma'am

NATASHA
Do you think you could give myself and Mr. Wanderdoff a chance to speak priwately?

LOUIE
Well, sure-diddily-do. I was about to make our afternoon coffee run anyway. Can I get you something a little fancy-dancier than our home brewed auto drip?

NATASHA
No, thank you.

LOUIE
Very well. And please, take your time with the screenplay.

NATASHA
Absolutely.

LOUIE
Uncle Harold, I'm going on a coffee run!

HAROLD
(Concerned with being alone with NATASHA)
Louie...

LOUIE
Tootles! *(LOUIE exits)*

(NATASHA drops the script in a nearby trash can. She moves closer and watches HAROLD for a bit)

NATASHA
You played my husband quite masterfully, Mr. Wanderdoff.

HAROLD
I'm not sure how to respond to that.

NATASHA
Just take the compliment. *(HAROLD nods and returns to 'work')* You're wery good, you know. I admire a man with skills.

(HAROLD nods and answers the phone)

HAROLD
Sell at 84. Tell Dickerson the C.E.O. is history. Yes, I have inside information.

(NATASHA unplugs the receiver near the base of

the phone and holds it up. *He doesn't notice and carries on his 'conversation'*)

HAROLD
Yes, absolutely. *(Laughs)* Well, if you say so. Why? Uh-huh. Yes. Go on. I'm listening. *(He turns as she releases the cord into him with a snap)* Hello? Hello? Guess we got cut off. *(Makes a show of seeing the cord)* Hey! How'd this happen?

NATASHA
(Moving in, seductively) Harold.

HAROLD
Yes?

NATASHA
You are quite the naughty boy, aren't you?

HAROLD
I…er…ah…naughty?

NATASHA
Don't be shy. Harold, there's something I need to tell you.

HAROLD
Please…There's really no need…

NATASHA
(She twirls a finger in his hair) I know it's a Ponzi scheme.

HAROLD
We can't, I'm married, and I love my – wait. What?

NATASHA
Your operation. I know it's a Ponzi scheme. I don't mind. In fact, I need it to be.

HAROLD
That is a baseless accusation, I have never –

NATASHA
(Putting a finger to his lips) Please. Let's not be childish. Here is what is going to happen. I need one hundred thousand dollars from you today. The rest of Dick's money is yours to keep.

HAROLD
Please, this makes no sense –

NATASHA
It doesn't need to.

HAROLD
What happens in three months when your husband comes back for his money?

NATASHA
He won't.

HAROLD
Why not?

NATASHA
That's what the hundred thousand is for.

(Beat)

HAROLD
I don't understand.

NATASHA
Don't you? *(Sighs)* My husband is a wery jealous man. He makes sure I don't have access to more than a few thousand dollars at any given time. He's afraid I'll fly off with a lover to Wenezwalla.

HAROLD
Where?

NATASHA
Wenezwalla, in South America.

HAROLD
Ah, I see. *(Still confused)* Wait —

NATASHA
I think we both agree, this world would be a better place without Dick Wellington. You heard his phone call. The man is ewil.

HAROLD
Well, maybe, but...

NATASHA
I need the hundred thousand to take care of this problem. I have someone coming from the motherland. Today. Ex-KGB. Wery subtle. Wery discreet.

HAROLD
You're not saying...?

NATASHA
Of course I am. I can't have the money being traced back to me when I rub Dick out.

HAROLD
Ahhh?

NATASHA
When Ed Thompson told me about his genius adwisor, I thought it sounded too good to be true. Then, after thinking about it, I hoped it was too good to be true. I had my man in Russia do a little research and woila! Here I am.

HAROLD
Listen, I can't possibly be a part of this –

NATASHA
You have no choice, Mr. Wanderdoff. If my calculations are correct, by the end of today, your accounts will be as empty as a beet shed during Borscht Fest. And you will be in jail by tomorrow. Probably Louie as well.

HAROLD
No. He didn't know anything about it.

NATASHA
Won't look that way. We can't have that, now can we? I will be back in one hour with my friend, Sergey. He will be expecting the hundred thousand dollars. He will, in no way, tolerate any deweeation from the plan. All you have to do is get me my money, and keep your mouth shut. That's not so hard, is it? *(She touches his face in a seductive way)*

HAROLD
Well, I –

NATASHA
(She slaps his face) I said to keep your mouth shut. *(Heading to the door)* I will see you in one hour. Do not wex me.

HAROLD
Sorry?

NATASHA
Wex! Wex! Do not wex me!

HAROLD
Vex, yes I see. No.

NATASHA
(NATASHA walks to the front door, then turns back) One hour. *(NATASHA exits)*

HAROLD
(HAROLD slowly sinks into a chair) Oh dear. I can't be part of this. *(He goes to the phone and dials)* Louie? Yes, I need you to go to the bank right now. Withdraw one hundred thousand dollars in cash and bring it here quickly. I'll explain later, just do it. And be ready to be on your toes. I need to figure out how to stop something. *(He hangs up and makes another call)* Phil? I want to you to put 900,000 in for Donnerby. I know it's big, spread it out. *(On computer)* Yes, I'm sending you the account number right now. Well, of course it's going to be difficult, but that's why you're the best, right? I know your people can handle these kinds of numbers. Done. Thanks, but I don't need luck. *(Hangs up)* I need a drink. *(He pours himself one and downs it. Ding dong)* Nope. Nuh-uh. Not going to face anybody else right now.

(Slightly unhinged laugh, then HAROLD marches out the upstage left door, and the door slam is simultaneous with GRAMPS' entrance from the kitchen, MR. WINKLES in his arms)

GRAMPS
Hey Louie, got a new one for ya… Where is everybody? *(Ding dong. GRAMPS cocks his ear. Did he hear something? Ding dong. Knocking. GRAMPS answers the phone)* Hello? *(More ding dongs and knocks. Could it be the door?)* Hold on to your pants, I've only got two legs here.

MR. WINKLES
Four, counting mine.

GRAMPS
I don't see you walking.

(GRAMPS opens the front door. Enter AGENT VIRGINIA SLADEMENGTON [pronounced SLADE-ming-ton], she is a matronly, buxom woman wearing cat eye glasses.. Although some might perceive her as past her prime, she would heartily disagree, as would GRAMPS. She is on the prowl for a new man in her life)

GRAMPS
(Taking in this stunning creature) Woah.

AGENT VIRGINIA SLADEMENGTON
Well, hello, handsome. I'm Agent Slademengton, Securities and Exchange Commission. I'm looking for Mr. Vanderdoff.

GRAMPS
I'm Mr. Vanderdoff.

AGENT VIRGINIA SLADEMENGTON
No, cutie, Harold Vanderdoff.

GRAMPS
(Ushering her in, intrigued by this beautiful creature) Come in, come in, Miss…?

AGENT VIRGINIA SLADEMENGTON
(Taking in MR. WINKLES) Oh, er, Slademengton.

GRAMPS
Miss O' Erslademengton?

AGENT VIRGINIA SLADEMENGTON
No, Slademengton.

GRAMPS
Noel Slademengton?

AGENT VIRGINIA SLADEMENGTON
Just Slademengton.

GRAMPS
Justina Slademengton?

AGENT VIRGINIA SLADEMENGTON
(Hitting him with her small purse) Stop that! You're teasing me. Virginia Slademengton.

GRAMPS
Virginia? Like the ham? I love ham.

AGENT VIRGINIA SLADEMENGTON
You stop. *(Hits him with her purse again)*

GRAMPS
(GRAMPS growls a bit and AGENT VIRGINIA SLADEMENGTON giggles) So, have you met Mr. Winkles here?

MR. WINKLES
Hi.

AGENT VIRGINIA SLADEMENGTON
Oooo! I simply adore ventriloquism. My late husband was a ventriloquist.

GRAMPS
You don't say!

AGENT VIRGINIA SLADEMENGTON
I do! Why don't you show me some of your material?

GRAMPS
Really?

AGENT VIRGINIA SLADEMENGTON
It would be my pleasure.

GRAMPS
Well Alrighty. Now I'm kinda nervous. Here we go!

MR. WINKLES
Say, whaddaya call a nosey pepper?

GRAMPS
I dunno. What?

MR. WINKLES
Jalapeño business! *(MR. WINKLES bobs his head back and forth)*

AGENT VIRGINIA SLADEMENGTON
(She laughs heartily. GRAMPS is delighted) Ha, I do declare, that is hilarious. And look, you gave him some head sass.

GRAMPS
I sure did!

AGENT VIRGINIA SLADEMENGTON
But I shouldn't mix so much pleasure with my business, I'm afraid I have a job to do. Can you kindly tell me where Harold Vanderdoff is?

GRAMPS
No idea.

AGENT VIRGINIA SLADEMENGTON
Is he not here?

GRAMPS
Could be.

MR. WINKLES
Would you like to have a seat?

AGENT VIRGINIA SLADEMENGTON
(Giggles) Thank you. That I would.

(HAROLD enters and heads straight to the bar, not noticing AGENT SLADEMENGTON)

GRAMPS
Harold, we have a –

HAROLD
Not now dad.

(He pours himself a drink and takes a sip)

AGENT VIRGINIA SLADEMENGTON
Harold Vanderdoff?

(HAROLD turns to see her holding up her badge. Spit take)

AGENT VIRGINIA SLADEMENGTON
Agent Virginia Slademengton, Securities and Exchange Commission.

HAROLD
Ha! Right! Yes! I was expecting you. To be here. Today. Yes.

AGENT VIRGINIA SLADEMENGTON
Well, dear, shall we get started? *(She opens her oversized bag and pulls out paperwork)*

(Enter LOUIE)

LOUIE
Hey Uncle Harold, I got the cash for you. I have to say, they sure looked at me cock-eyed, pardon my French, when I asked for a hundred thousand in cash.

(AGENT SLADEMENGTON is immediately

suspicious)

HAROLD
Ah, yes. Louie, have you met Agent Sleddymentionson?

AGENT VIRGINIA SLADEMENGTON
Slademengton.

HAROLD
Exactly.

LOUIE
(Bright and chipper) Ah! Pleased to meetcha!

HAROLD
She's from the S.E.C.

LOUIE
(Shaking her hand, then suddenly catching on that it might be a bad thing to have a S.E.C. agent in the house) Ah-ha-ha-hah. How are you?

AGENT VIRGINIA SLADEMENGTON
Oh, fine, thank you. Are you an employee of Vanderdoff Investments?

HAROLD
Employee?

AGENT VIRGINIA SLADEMENGTON
Yes, in your wealth management business?

HAROLD
Oh, I merely help out a few family and friends with investing. I would hardly call it a business.

AGENT VIRGINIA SLADEMENGTON
Oh, dear, I see. My mistake. *(Consulting her paperwork)* If it's not a business, why do you need

to rent an office?

HAROLD
(Holds up his hands to indicate the room) Well, we're not in an office now, are we?

LOUIE
Touche! *(HAROLD gives LOUIE a small kick)*

HAROLD
My wife, Judith, likes to have the place to herself during the day, so I rented a little office for myself.

AGENT VIRGINIA SLADEMENGTON
Yes, I also see that she's a substantial investor in your business.

HAROLD
I do help to manage her money as well. *(HAROLD looks at his watch)*

LOUIE
Could I offer you a drink, Agent Slawdmandingo?

AGENT VIRGINIA SLADEMENGTON
A tad early for me, thanks, sugar.

(Real phone rings, and HAROLD is glad for the excuse to stop talking to AGENT SLADEMENGTON again)

HAROLD
Excuse me one moment. *(Answers phone)* Ahoy-ahoy? *(Yikes)* Oh, hello, O'Donnell.

LOUIE
O'Donnell? *(Looking at his watch)* Oh, that's right, we just missed the fight. *(To AGENT SLADEMENGTON)* O'Donnell has been the

mixed martial arts champ two years running! *(He rushes over and turns on the TV. We hear the post game commentary about the fight)*

COMEMNTATOR 1 ON TV
Ladies and gentlemen, that's it! O'Donnell came out on top again!

LOUIE
Winner and still champ-pee-on, O'Donnell!

HAROLD
Quiet down Louie!

COMENTATOR 2 ON TV
And here's the stretcher. Oh dear that's never good. Let's look at that instant replay of the Match-Ending-Move. (Sound of bones crunching)

LOUIE
Oh my goodness! They'll never walk again!

COMEMNTATOR 1 ON TV
Horrific to be sure. The body brace is going on now, and doctors are prepping the ER for —

HAROLD
Louie!

LOUIE
Sorry. *(Turns off TV)*

HAROLD
(Into phone) Congratulations, Champ. No, no. Of course you can, it's the end of the quarter. *(Casually, but with secret hopes)* Or you could just let it automatically roll over again. *(Reacts to phone yelling we can't hear)* What? I have never ducked you at the end of a quarter. You stopped by the office before the big fight? Yes, I'm sure

that was frustrating. No, the office is closed. I see. You're already on your way here? There's really no need...hello? Hello? *(Hangs up)* Ah, yes, where were we?

AGENT VIRGINIA SLADEMENGTON
I was questioning you, m'dear.

HAROLD
Of course.

AGENT VIRGINIA SLADEMENGTON
Your return rate is so much higher than the standard interest rates for short-term credit. So maybe I can help you here, dear: why don't you take out loans? The interest you'd pay the bank would be much less than you would ever have to pay investors.

LOUIE
Wow. I never thought to ask that.

HAROLD
Two reasons, really. First and foremost, I am helping my friends, not just myself. Secondly, if the banks fully understand what I'm doing, they could feasibly replicate it. I prefer to keep the banks at arm's length.

LOUIE
(Nervously trying to help) And better your length of arm than mine, because my arms are shorter. Ha!

AGENT VIRGINIA SLADEMENGTON
(Producing more paperwork) Mr. Vanderdoff, why the confidentiality agreements? Why on earth would you need such secrecy?

HAROLD
Simple: I need to protect what I do. There is a finite amount of money to be made in this area of business. The pie cannot feed everyone.

LOUIE
Ooh, I love pie. Especially rhubarb pie.

GRAMPS
Did someone say pie?

MR. WINKLES
Pie?

ALL
Yum!

HAROLD
Thank you everyone.

MR. WINKLES
Wait, seriously, pie?

HAROLD
Why don't you shut your piehole?

AGENT VIRGINIA SLADEMENGTON
Mr. Vanderdoff! There's no reason to be rude to your father!

HAROLD
I was talking to the dummy!

GRAMPS
Hey....

AGENT VIRGINIA SLADEMENGTON
I can't abide rudeness, Mr. Vanderdoff. Now see here: Your system of options buying and selling seems to have no correlation to actual market fluctuation.

LOUIE
Now that's a good point.

AGENT VIRGINIA SLADEMENGTON
Explain yourself, mister!

HAROLD
Ah yes, well, say hypothetically, if someone was only to invest in a handful of companies that he knew very well, he could, without any insider trading, mind you, have a good idea of when things may be heading south, and be able to bet against those possible futures.

AGENT VIRGINIA SLADEMENGTON
What could you possibly know so well, inside and out, that you could invest in, without it being insider trading?

LOUIE
Panda Fest. As an example.

AGENT VIRGINIA SLADEMENGTON
Excuse me?

HAROLD
Yes, thank you, Louie. I am so glad you are here to help with this. Agent Sleighbellsring –

AGENT VIRGINIA SLADEMENGTON
Slademengton.

HAROLD
Yes, quite. In the attic, I have records of every day of trading I've ever done since I started. Perhaps you would care to peruse those records?

AGENT VIRGINIA SLADEMENGTON
I would, Mr. Vanderdoff. And I will. With a fine-tooth comb.

HAROLD
They are clearly marked by year. My father would be happy to show you to the attic.

LOUIE
Gramps!

GRAMPS
What?

LOUIE
Could you show this lady how to get to the attic?

GRAMPS
You know I could! *(To AGENT VIRGINIA SLADEMENGTON)* I would be honored to escort you upstairs. May I call you Virginia?

AGENT VIRGINIA SLADEMENGTON
You may.

HAROLD
Ooh! May I also call you Vir-

AGENT VIRGINIA SLADEMENGTON
You may not.

HAROLD
Yes. Of course. Thank you.

AGENT VIRGINIA SLADEMENGTON
(To GRAMPS) You're not planning to get fresh with me in the attic are you?

GRAMPS
Madam, I shall be a perfect gentleman.

AGENT VIRGINIA SLADEMENGTON
(Disappointed) Suit yourself. *(They giggle and start to exit)*

HAROLD
Maybe you could show her some of your routines!

GRAMPS
You know it!

(GRAMPS and AGENT SLADEMENGTON exit, upstairs)

HAROLD
That should keep her busy for a while.

LOUIE
(Sotto voce) What's going on? I thought you said you never did any investing?

HAROLD
I didn't.

LOUIE
But you just sent her upstairs to look at your trading records.

HAROLD
I did.

LOUIE
I have two words for that maneuver, and they're both "coo". *(Beat)* Coo-coo!

HAROLD
Listen, years ago, I started making records of trades I should have done, combined with cryptic notes, meaningless numbers and glowing thank you letters, in case I was audited by the S.E.C. It will take her hours to get through it all, and she'll learn nothing. The closest thing I have to incriminating paperwork is at the office. But even in that, I refer to myself as Advisor X, and never use my own name. And all of that is safely

locked up in my office.

LOUIE
What do you mean safely locked up? You don't even have a key.

HAROLD
Hey! Locked up is locked up. Don't look a gift horse in the mouth.

LOUIE
What are we gonna do?

HAROLD
Not panic, for starters.

LOUIE
I'm not good at that.

HAROLD
I've noticed. *(Grabs a hammer)* Listen, next time you think you have something helpful to say to that S.E.C. agent *(Hands LOUIE the hammer)*, apply this to your head liberally.

LOUIE
I don't see how that will help.

HAROLD
Really? Try it.

(Car Arrives. GRAMPS comes running downstairs)

GRAMPS
O'Donnell's here! I saw the champ out the window! Woo-hoo! O'Donnell! O'Donnell! O'Donnell!

HAROLD
Dad, I really must insist you quiet down. We're trying to conduct business here.

GRAMPS
But it's O'Donnell! Woo!

HAROLD
Quiet! You know, assisted living is really not out of my price range.

GRAMPS
Alright son, that's strike three. You may be too old to put over my knee, but you need to be taken down a peg.

HAROLD
Fine.

(Ding dong)

HAROLD
(To LOUIE) Okay, I have to talk O'Donnell into rolling the money over. We can't let the champ take any money out until the Donnerby investment pays off. Let me do all the talking. Don't say a single word.

LOUIE
But –

HAROLD
Not a single word! No matter what happens! Not a single word! Say it!

LOUIE
I will not say a single word. I swear.

(HAROLD opens the door, and there stands O'DONNELL, the women's mixed martial arts champ, still in her fight gear: sports bra with logo, shorts, open-fingered fight gloves, tall lace-up boots, and an open robe over the whole shebang. She has some interesting body tattoos. She's a knockout.

She punches HAROLD in the face and he goes down like a sack of potatoes. He's out cold. LOUIE so wants to say something, but has clearly been told 'not a single word'. He waves. He attempts to communicate without words for a bit. Finally)

LOUIE
Ahhh, oowah, odeeeo?

O'DONNELL
Where's me money?

LOUIE
Whaaaa-oh mmmmmder?

O'DONNELL
You making fun of me? *(She picks up LOUIE and holds him against a wall)* Harold has ducked me five quarters straight!

(Meanwhile, GRAMPS has fetched the ice bucket from the bar and uses it to revive HAROLD. GRAMPS then helps HAROLD to his feet, behind O'DONNELL)

O'DONNELL
Well not this time! Do you think me an eejit? Givin' me a divil a one? I've had it up to here with this malarky. You hear me?

(GRAMPS has now lined up a dazed HAROLD behind O'DONNELL and he gives her a shove. When she turns around, GRAMPS is pointing to HAROLD with an 'I can't believe he just pushed you' face. She roundhouse kicks HAROLD in the head, sending him to be awkwardly sprawled out on the sofa. GRAMPS is elated. More shadow boxing)

O'DONNELL
You're killing me Harold! I needed that money for me Da, ya knacker! You broke me heart! *(To LOUIE)* You think that's how friends should treat each other?

(LOUIE shakes his head 'no'. In the meantime, GRAMPS grabs the seltzer bottle from the bar and uses it to revive Harold by spraying bursts in his face. HAROLD finally rises and stumbles behind O'DONNELL again. She is alternating between shouting at LOUIE and shaking him like you should never shake a baby)

O'DONNELL
Duckin' out on them when they come to claim their money? Jeannie Mac! Is that how you treat a pal? Abandon them in their time of need? Huh? Answer me that!

(Seeing a golden opportunity, GRAMPS sprays O'DONNELL in the back of the head, then tosses the bottle to HAROLD, who unwittingly catches it. Slow burn as O'DONNELL turns. Looking at the bottle in his hands, HAROLD realizes what this must look like just as GRAMPS seizes the bottle from him)

GRAMPS
Harold! That's not nice!

O'DONNELL
GRRRHHHH! *(She puts HAROLD through a punishing series of grappling moves and body slams. GRAMPS finds this terrifically amusing. LOUIE is horrified. GRAMPS intermittently sprays HAROLD in the face with the seltzer bottle*

as the opportunity presents itself)

GRAMPS
(Spray!) I told you you'd get yours! *(Spray!)* Three Strikes!

(O'DONNELL flips HAROLD. LOUIE simply can't take it anymore. He grabs the money he got from the bank and holds it out to O'DONNELL)

LOUIE
Here, take it, take it!

O'DONNELL
Is that me money?

LOUIE
Yes. No. Well, maybe. Yes.

O'DONNELL
(Looking in the bag) All hundred thousand?

LOUIE
Exactly.

(GRAMPS has gone to the bar and is recharging the seltzer bottle)

O'DONNELL
It better be, ya langer, or I'll be back. *(Starts to exit, opens door, turns back)* You know, Harold, you really hurt me! *(O'DONNELL exits. Door slam)*

LOUIE
Uncle Harold? Uncle Harold? Are you alright? *(HAROLD is out of it – a dazed mess on the floor)*

GRAMPS
Three strikes and he's out.

LOUIE
Gramps, what are you doing?

GRAMPS
Reloading.

(GRAMPS has just finished and walks back to where HAROLD is lying on the floor. He sprays him in the face. HAROLD leaps to his feet)

GRAMPS
That go the way ya thought it would?

(HAROLD opens his mouth to protest, but every time he does, GRAMPS sprays him in mouth. A chase ensues, HAROLD stumbling after GRAMPS, GRAMPS giggling with glee, hitting HAROLD with more bursts of seltzer)

GRAMPS
Weeeeeeeeeeeeeeeeeeeeeee!

(Finally, GRAMPS runs out and HAROLD gives up)

HAROLD
(Trying to catch his breath) He's pretty fast for an old guy.

LOUIE
Are you okay?

HAROLD
I've been better. I'm certainly going to feel that in the morning. How'd you get her to stop? *(He goes to make himself a drink)*

LOUIE
I gave her the money.

HAROLD
What money?

LOUIE
The hundred thousand dollars from the bank.

HAROLD
(HAROLD slams down the bottle. Slowly he turns)
You what?

LOUIE
I gave her the money.

(HAROLD picks up the metal tray from the bar and methodically hits himself in the face a few times, then he goes to the desk and retrieves a pad and pencil and hands them to LOUIE)

HAROLD
Here. Why don't you get a head start on writing my eulogy? *(He sinks to the couch, or a chair)*

LOUIE
Why? We still have the 900,000 for the Donnerby investment.

HAROLD
I know. It's invested.

LOUIE
Then what did you need the hundred thousand for?

HAROLD
To help me stall Natasha.

(Doorbell rings. LOUIE, near the door, opens it before hearing HAROLD's protest)

HAROLD
No, wait –

(Too late. The door is open and in step NATASHA and SERGEY. He looks like a nasty piece of work. Long black leather jacket and sunglasses)

NATASHA
Hello, boys.

(SERGEY cracks his knuckles in a menacing way. Blackout)

END OF ACT ONE

ACT II

(Lights up, we go back in time a couple of seconds)

NATASHA
Hello, boys. *(SERGEY cracks his knuckles in a menacing way)* Harold, this is my friend Sergey Kalashnikov.

LOUIE
Sir Gay Kalashnikov? *(Sotto voce to HAROLD)* He's probably Russian royalty. *(LOUIE makes with an elaborate bow)* Sir Gay! May I please to have the honor of presenting unto you, my name in verbal form, Louie Vanderdoff of the local Vanderdoffs. *(More elaborate bowing)*

SERGEY
(To NATASHA) What is he doing?

NATASHA
(Confused) I don't know.

LOUIE
(To SERGEY) Sir Gay *(Small bow)* Your

Lordshipness, may I pourith unto you some vodka of thine motherland?

SERGEY
You may.

LOUIE
(Heading to the bar) And for your Consortina?

SERGEY
(To NATASHA) I think he means you.

NATASHA
No, we can't stay long. Harold, I believe you have something for us?

HAROLD
Yes. *(He doesn't move)*

NATASHA
May we have it?

HAROLD
Yeeee-es. *(Still doesn't move)*

NATASHA
Harold is there something wrong?

HAROLD
Well...

(Suddenly, the front door bursts open and in storms DICK WELLINGTON)

DICK WELLINGTON
Ah-Ha! I knew it!

LOUIE
Sir, you can't –

DICK WELLINGTON
Sit down!

LOUIE
(Quickly sits) Okay.

DICK WELLINGTON
Thought you could get away with it, huh? Thought I wouldn't figure it out?

NATASHA
Now, Dickie –

DICK WELLINGTON
Don't Dickie me! If I want to hear from you, I'll pull your string so you can tell us how hard math is! I know exactly what's going on around here! You can't pull the wool over my eyes!

NATASHA
Oh dear –

DICK
You brought your Russian boyfriend here, over to Vanderdoff's place as a tryst-house to satisfy your insatiable lust!

NATASHA
What? No, this is my second cousin Sergey Kalashnikov from Novosibirsk.

LOUIE
(Gasps, then sotto voce to HAROLD) That must mean she's royalty, too. *(To NATASHA)* Your Ladyshipness, forgiveth me. *(He goes into the 'I'm a little tea pot' pose and begins to slowly bend over)* It was not beknown unto me of your status-ship.

DICK WELLINGTON
What's wrong with him?

HAROLD
Everything.

NATASHA
Darling, I –

DICK WELLINGTON
Darling what? I suppose you were going to tell me that your cousin here is also interested in investing.

NATASHA
He is.

DICK WELLINGTON
Please. I can see right through you. You and *(Indicating everyone in the room)* your menagerie of lovers! You make me sick!

(In the meantime, SERGEY has grabbed the frying pan GRAMPS ate his eggs from earlier. He bonks DICK on the back of the head. DICK holds stiff and upright for a moment, then over he goes. His eyes remain open)

LOUIE
Cheese and rice! That's no way for a nobleman to behave, striking commoners! *(Sees the bar is out of ice)* I'll go get some ice!

(LOUIE exits to kitchen. SERGEY bends down to check DICK's pulse)

HAROLD
Is he alive?

SERGEY
For now. *(He pulls out a gun and starts to screw a silencer onto it)*

HAROLD
(Horrified) What, no! Not here!

SERGEY
Why not?

HAROLD
Because it's my house! *(This doesn't seem to impress SERGEY. HAROLD suddenly remembers a reason SERGEY might care about)* And, there's an S.E.C. agent upstairs as we speak!

SERGEY
Should I kill him first?

HAROLD and NATASHA
NO!

HAROLD
(To NATASHA) Is this what you call very subtle? Very discreet?!

NATASHA
This wasn't the plan. I didn't know my husband would follow me here!

(Meanwhile, SERGEY has produced a rubber topped medicine bottle and a syringe. He pokes it into the bottle, fills it, and gives DICK a shot of it)

HAROLD
AHHH! What is that? Poison?

SERGEY
No, Panzadrine. It will keep him paralyzed for an hour or two.

(He leaves the bottle and syringe on a side table. During the following conversation, SERGEY props DICK up on the sofa and considers what to do with him. He adjusts DICK's wig back and forth a few times)

HAROLD
Then what?

SERGEY
He'll recover fully. No side effects.

HAROLD
Oh, good.

SERGEY
We'll take him with us and dispose of him.

HAROLD
Wait...

(LOUIE returns with an old fashioned, screw top ice bag)

LOUIE
How's he doing? Is he alright? *(He places the ice bag on DICK's head, like a saggy hat)*

SERGEY
(Pointing to the ice bag) What is that supposed to do?

HAROLD
Strip him of his dignity would be my guess.

NATASHA
Listen, Louie, we're going to take Dick to the hospital. *(Getting HAROLD and SERGEY to play along)* Right?

HAROLD
(Unsure of what to do, decides to play along) Right.

SERGEY
Why not? Let's go with that. Do you have an old rug?

HAROLD
What say?

SERGEY
To wrap him up in.

HAROLD
Of course. That's sensible. *(To LOUIE)* Louie, I need you to take Sergey here down to the basement and drag one of those old rugs up here so we can wrap *(Indicating DICK)* him up in it.

LOUIE
Why would we do that?

HAROLD
(Indignant) MY GOD MAN! Can't you see he's in shock? We need to keep him warm!

LOUIE
Then why don't we wrap him in a blanket?

HAROLD
(Furious) Because rugs are warmer than blankets! That is a scientific fact! Everyone knows that!

SERGEY
I didn't know that.

LOUIE
Then why did you ask for a rug?

HAROLD
Come on, Let's go!

(Harold escorts SERGEY off into basement. LOUIE lingers by Dick Wellington)

HAROLD
(At basement door) Louie! Hurry and get the rug! There's no time, there's no TIME!

LOUIE
(after false exit) They're kinda buried under a bunch of stuff and junk.

HAROLD
Then unbury them, chop, chop! *(He pushes LOUIE off and slams the basement door)*

NATASHA
I have a car in the driweway. We'll throw him in the trunk and be off.

HAROLD
Off?

NATASHA
Off to knock him off.

HAROLD
Off, off?

NATASHA
You don't want to know.

HAROLD
Wait! Now, although that seems like a good plan on the surface, I think, maybe, we should hide him in the basement. At least until that S.E.C. agent is gone.

NATASHA
You make a good point. *(HAROLD is relieved)* Where's the money?

HAROLD
(So much for relief) Where's the what?

NATASHA
The money.

HAROLD
What money?

NATASHA
The hundred thousand dollars.

HAROLD
Oh, the money! Specifically, you meant that money. Yes. Of course.

(AGENT SLADEMENGTON has come walking down the stairs)

AGENT VIRGINIA SLADEMENGTON
Yes, the money, that's the question isn't it, Mr. Vanderdoff. When you follow the money, you always find -

(Everyone freezes as AGENT SLADEMENGTON sees DICK WELLINGTON on the sofa, eyes open with an ice bag on his head. Terrible pause)

AGENT VIRGINIA SLADEMENGTON
Dick Wellington?

HAROLD
Yes.

AGENT VIRGINIA SLADEMENGTON
Of Wellington Worldwide Empire Industries?

HAROLD
Yes.

AGENT VIRGINIA SLADEMENGTON
Dick Wellington, we meet again. I should have known your crooked fingers were knuckle deep in- *(Notices he is frozen. She waves her hand in front of his face. To HAROLD)* What's he doing?

HAROLD
What isn't he doing? Thinking, planning, resting – all at the same time! Remarkable.

AGENT VIRGINIA SLADEMENGTON
What ever do you mean?

HAROLD
This is how he gets his great ideas! He goes into a sort of trance, then suddenly, when you least expect it – BAM! – the big ideas happen!

AGENT VIRGINIA SLADEMENGTON
I've been investigating Dick Wellington for years and have never heard of such a thing.

HAROLD
Ha! Ha! Ha! Dick Wellington likes to keep it private! Right, Natasha?

NATASHA
Right.

HAROLD
This is his wife, Natasha.

AGENT VIRGINIA SLADEMENGTON
Ah, the newest wife. How do you do?

HAROLD
She does fine. Now perhaps we should just let–

AGENT VIRGINIA SLADEMENGTON
What's on his head?

HAROLD
Ice pack.

AGENT VIRGINIA SLADEMENGTON
Why?

HAROLD
His brain gets hot when he thinks.

NATASHA
Wery, wery, hot.

(HAROLD adjusts the ice bag, and as a consequence, DICK's wig a little bit. AGENT SLADEMENGTON moves in for a closer inspection, as LOUIE enters from the basement, carrying the front end of the rolled up rug. HAROLD rushes over to him)

HAROLD
Louie! *(Grabs him, pushes the rug back down into the basement. We hear SERGEY fall down the stairs as HAROLD slams the door shut. Sotto voce to LOUIE)* You have to play along with whatever I say, get it?

LOUIE
Got it.

HAROLD
Good. *(To the room, explaining to LOUIE)* I was just telling Agent Schadenfreud here –

AGENT VIRGINIA SLADEMENGTON
Slademengton.

HAROLD
– Precisely – how Dick Wellington goes into his "thinking trances".

LOUIE
(Nods his head, playing along) Yes, you were. *(HAROLD gives him a look)*

AGENT VIRGINIA SLADEMENGTON
Oh, dear me, he looks like he's had a stroke.

HAROLD
OF GENIUS! I agree. Fascinating, the way his mind works. Well, we had better let him get back to it, don't you think? What can I do for you, Agent Slayingten?

AGENT VIRGINIA SLADEMENGTON
I had some questions about your paperwork.

HAROLD
Then by all means, let's go look at it *(trying to get AGENT SLADEMENGTON upstairs)*

AGENT VIRGINIA SLADEMENGTON
(Pointing at DICK) Are you sure we should –

HAROLD
Absolutely, see, when Dick Wellington forms his idea, whatever it may be, what companies to take over, what markets he should exploit, what-have-you, he literally bursts out of this state, and you do not want to be here when that happens. It can get pretty messy.

AGENT VIRGINIA SLADEMENGTON
Messy?

(HAROLD frantically extemporizes a series of gestures that would make a mess of the room, including the spewing of fluids, rude sounds, and what-not, then ends with holding his nose. AGENT SLADEMENGTON is speechless. HAROLD escorts AGENT SLADEMENGTON towards the stairs)

HAROLD
Let's go look at that paperwork! *(Whispers over his shoulder to LOUIE as he exits)* Louie, you have to stand up and be a man. She can't come

back and see Dick like this.

AGENT VIRGINIA SLADEMENGTON
Mr. Vanderdoff!

HAROLD
Coming! *(To LOUIE)* You know what to do!

LOUIE
(Thinking outloud) Pretty messy... *(Getting into character)* I'm Dick Wellington... *(LOUIE, as DICK WELLINGTON, starts running around the room, making a terrible mess of everything)*

NATASHA
(After a bit) What are you doing?

LOUIE
You heard Uncle Harold: we have to make it look like... *(LOUIE repeats the sounds and gestures HAROLD used. He then continues making a mess. SERGEY enters from the basement. LOUIE gives him a quick curtsy)* Your Lordshipness. *(He gets back to work)*

SERGEY
(Rubbing his neck from the fall) What's going on?

NATASHA
That S.E.C. agent was in here. She saw Dickie.

SERGEY
What happened?

NATASHA
Harold conwinced her Dickie was thinking, then managed to get her upstairs.

SERGEY
Not bad. *(Indicating LOUIE)* What's he doing?

NATASHA
I'm not sure. Louie! Help us get him to the basement!

LOUIE
Why?

NATASHA
Because it's warmer down there?

LOUIE
No, no! We have to play along with Uncle Harold's story! Okay, so after he had his big idea, next came the big mess. Then what happened?

SERGEY
We should get him to the car!

LOUIE
No. *(Almost laughing at the idea that he could ever be wrong about this)* I think I know what Uncle Harold wants us to do. *(Suddenly serious)* Ok. What I'm thinking in my head – *(Pointing to his head)* because that's where I think – is that he had the idea, and then… *(He grabs a bottle of booze and slops it on DICK)* got drunk to celebrate! Then… *(He pushes DICK over)* he passed out!

SERGEY
And now he lies with Weenus.

LOUIE
I'm sorry?

SERGEY
(As if it's as clear as day) Now he lies with Weenus.

(Beat)

LOUIE
One more time.

SERGEY
He lies with Weenus, Weenus, the Roman goddess of love and sleep.

NATASHA
(That can't be right) Sleep?

LOUIE
Right. Ok, so what else happened?

SERGEY
(SERGEY's starting to like this game) Right, so… *(Grabs another bottle of booze and sprinkles it on DICK)* he was drinking…and, uh, we don't need this *(Takes the ice bag and throws it across the room, adjusts DICK's wig a few more times, to his liking)* Then, he loosen [sic] his tie… *(He loosens DICK's tie, then, noticing the bowl of peanuts on the bar)* Wait, I know! Put peenus on his face!

LOUIE
I beg your pardon?

(Beat)

SERGEY
Put peenus on his face.

(Beat)

LOUIE
One more time.

SERGEY
Put peenus all over his face.

LOUIE
(Calmly) Now I am open to any and all suggestions, and I want to foster a collaborative, creative environment here, but I really fail to see how that

might help.

SERGEY
Peenus! PEE-NUS! *(Grabbing a jar of peanuts)* Dry roasted peenus! *(Pours them on Dick's head)* That's what I eat when I am drunk.

LOUIE
Well, yes, I see. I didn't...Ok. Good job.

NATASHA
Enough of this! Sergey, go get that rug.

SERGEY
(Put off that he can no longer play the game) Fine! *(SERGEY exits to the basement)*

LOUIE
Did you know he meant peanuts?

NATASHA
Of course.

LOUIE
Then why didn't you say something?

NATASHA
What do you mean?

LOUIE
Cause it didn't sound like peanuts to me?

NATASHA
What did it sound like to you?

LOUIE
Well, it sounded... it sorta sounded... I thought... never mind. We have to finish!

NATASHA
Finish what?

(LOUIE repeats the sounds and gestures HAROLD made to show the mess. He rushes around making last minute adjustments to DICK: loosening DICK's tie, putting a glass in his hand, a cigar in his mouth, sunglasses on his face, then puts a New Year's Eve party hat on his head. He puts a scotch bottle in one of DICK'S hands and peanuts in his other hand)

LOUIE
Have some more peenus.

(LOUIE admires his work. Enter HAROLD down the stairs, with AGENT SLADEMENGTON close behind. HAROLD walks with confidence, knowing full well he has given them enough time to get DICK out of the room – at least that's taken care of)

HAROLD
I hope that explains everything, Agent Sla – ha – Ah – Wha…? What's happening now?

LOUIE
(Proud of his work) Well, you were right! He had his big idea and *(Repeats 'messy' gesture)* and then we had some drinks to celebrate, and we were having the rootinest, tootinest good old time, and Dick here finished the scotch, drank the rest of the watermelon schnapps, and passed right out.

NATASHA
But before that, he ate some peenus.

AGENT VIRGINIA SLADEMENGTON
(Offended) What?

NATASHA
You can clearly see, he was getting all sloppy with

his peenus.

LOUIE
Peanuts.

NATASHA
Right.

(LOUIE beams at HAROLD, then gives him a subtle 'you can thank me later' nod. Pause)

AGENT VIRGINIA SLADEMENGTON
Mercy me. And all this happened in the few minutes we were out of the room?

HAROLD
(Finally snapping out of his stupor) Of course! Dick Wellington thinks large and he likes to live large. Good times! I'm actually sorry we missed the party.

AGENT VIRGINIA SLADEMENGTON
Listen Mr. Vanderdoff, there's something unusually screwy going on around here. I'm not buying your line of credit. First, you send me upstairs to go through those useless, "so-called", trading records that don't tell me a thing. For all I know, you just created boxes and boxes of paperwork indicating trades you should have made, in order to slow me down.

LOUIE
(Astonished) She's good.

AGENT VIRGINIA SLADEMENGTON
Sit down.

LOUIE
(Sits) Okay.

AGENT VIRGINIA SLADEMENGTON
Then comes all this nonsense with Dick Wellington here. I mean really! You can't fool me. I have a woman's intuition. I think there's something much more sinister going on here.

HAROLD
Whatever do you mean?

AGENT VIRGINIA SLADEMENGTON
Please. I'm an experienced field agent. I know exactly what is going on with Dick Wellington here. *(She props DICK back up on the couch)* You have clearly had a wax figure made of Dick Wellington in a pathetic attempt to intimidate me.

HAROLD
Come again?

AGENT VIRGINIA SLADEMENGTON
Since he weaseled his way out of so many S.E.C. charges, you thought I would be intimidated. But look at this thing: *(Disgusted)* It's not even that well made! *(Tapping with her pencil eraser on various parts of DICK's face as she talks about them)* This terrible skin tone. Look at that. And here? Bags under his eyes. Whatever this thing is, here. *(She uses his pencil to pull DICK's lips back in various ways, to show off the teeth)* These latex lips are impressive, but these ridiculous yellow teeth? I mean seriously. What do you take me for? *(Pulls off DICK's wig, shakes it in HAROLD's face)* And you didn't even bother to secure this ludicrous wig to its head in any sort of believable manner! *(Haphazardly tosses the wig back on top of DICK's head. She pick up a stapler from the coffee table and staples the wig

to DICK'S head. The group reacts) Did you really think you could fool me? As if someone of Dick Wellington's stature would be coming over to your house to do his "catatonic thinking"?

LOUIE
Ma'am, I assure you, that is Dick Wellington.

HAROLD
Oh, Louie, why bother? She's figured us out.

AGENT VIRGINIA SLADEMENGTON
Now, I'm here to find out more about your so-called investments. *(To LOUIE)* Earlier, you mentioned Koala Fest.

LOUIE
Panda Fest!

AGENT VIRGINIA SLADEMENGTON
Same difference.

LOUIE
(Highly offended) Ma'am! Koalas are, in no way, shape, or form, the noble panda! Don't get me started on koalas!

HAROLD
Seriously, don't.

LOUIE
Given half a chance, koalas would eat you, and everyone you love! The dastardly koala should be wiped off the face of the planet!

HAROLD
Louie, she didn't mean to upset you –

LOUIE
I don't give a shoot!

HAROLD
Louie, enough!

LOUIE
My dander has been raised, madam!

HAROLD
Louie! *(Making claw hands)* POLAR BEARS!

LOUIE
(Shrieks, and quickly sits) I'll be good. *(He sucks his thumb, and holds his ear)*

AGENT VIRGINIA SLADEMENGTON
Where, pray tell, is the rest of your record keeping, Mr. Vanderdoff?

HAROLD
I'm pretty sure it's all in the attic?

AGENT VIRGINIA SLADEMENGTON
Might there be anything at your office?

HAROLD
Well, there may be. Feel free to go down there and look around.

AGENT VIRGINIA SLADEMENGTON
Perhaps I will. Now if you will excuse me, I'm going to step out onto your porch and make a few calls to headquarters. Maybe see about a search warrant. There's always a paper trail, and I intend to find it. Tick-tock goes the clock. It's only a matter of time before I find out absolutely everything about Vanderdoff Investments. *(Exits)*

HAROLD
Good luck getting into that office. *(To LOUIE)* Louie, go tell Sergey the coast is clear for now, and help him get that rug up here.

LOUIE
Check! *(LOUIE exits to basement)*

HAROLD
(To NATASHA) Quick!

(NATASHA follows his lead and they get DICK upright and walk him one leg at a time to center, then lay him down on the floor in his 'dead bug' position, hands and feet in the air. HAROLD steps over him and pushes his legs down, which makes DICK sit up with his face in HAROLD'S crotch. HAROLD pushes DICK back down, which makes his feet kick HAROLD in the butt)

NATASHA
(An idea) Ah!

(NATASHA leads and pulls one arm straight as HAROLD pulls the opposite leg straight. They move on to the next limb, but as NATASHA pulls the arm and HAROLD pulls the leg, the limbs they just straightened out retract back to 'dead bug'. Repeat)

NATASHA
(New idea) Ah!

(NATASHA puts her foot on the hand that's down and pulls the other, as HAROLD holds down the leg that's down as he pulls on the other. Success! Beat. DICK snaps back to 'dead bug' position, startling NATASHA and HAROLD)

NATASHA and HAROLD
(Startled) Yah!

(LOUIE and SERGEY enter with rug. SERGEY sees DICK and makes an annoyed sound. He feels

around DICK'S torso with one hand, the hits his hand with the other. DICK straightens out. They proceed to roll DICK up in the rug)

LOUIE
Why are we tying him up?

NATASHA
To keep him warm!

LOUIE
Of course, of course.

(They finally manage to tie it shut)

HAROLD
There we are, snug as a bug in a rug.

SERGEY
Can we get him out the window? *(With SERGEY forcefully taking the lead, they move him to the window upstage of the couch)*

LOUIE
(While carrying the rug) Why don't we take him out the front door?

HAROLD
We can't let that agent see Dick rolled up in a rug.

LOUIE
How come?

HAROLD
Why do you have to ask so many questions?!

(They set the rug upstage of the couch. Unseen by the audience, it is pushed through an open hole on the upstage wall, and now the actor playing DICK can change to GRAMPS. When next they pick up 'Dick in a rug', it is a double with a dummy inside.

HAROLD opens the window and peers out. He quickly retracts his head and closes the window)

HAROLD
Bother! Agent whatsherjunk can see us from the porch.

NATASHA
How about the back door?

HAROLD
No good, my Dad will see us, and he can't keep his mouth shut about anything.

SERGEY
What about an upstairs window? We could drop him over the side of the building.

HAROLD
No, she could see it from the porch...BUT, we could hide him upstairs until the coast is clear.

NATASHA
Fine.

HAROLD
(To group) Help me!

(Lazzi ensues as they bang 'Dick in a rug' into various objects and walls, drop him and lift him, etc)

HAROLD
We'll never get him up the stairs. Maybe we should try the basement. *(More lazzi)*

SERGEY
Enough! I am not lifting a finger until I see my money.

HAROLD
What?

NATASHA
Give him his money!

HAROLD
(Pretending he can't hear well) I'm sorry?

SERGEY
(Losing patience) The hundred thousand dollars!

LOUIE
Oh, the hundred thousand dollars?

SERGEY
Da.

LOUIE
I gave it to Mary O'Donnell, the mixed martial arts champ.

(Beat)

SERGEY
You did what with the who now?

LOUIE
She was demanding her investment back, so I gave her the hundred thousand dollars in cash.

(Terrible pause)

HAROLD
Louie! Why didn't you tell me?!

LOUIE
What?

HAROLD
I can't believe you did that! How dare you?!

LOUIE
But I told –

HAROLD
I'm going to give you such a spanking!

(HAROLD grabs LOUIE and gives him 'such a spanking')

SERGEY
(SERGEY grabs HAROLD) Where is my money, little man?

LOUIE
You leave my uncle alone! *(SERGEY snarls at LOUIE)* Yipes! *(LOUIE exits quickly, into the kitchen)*

SERGEY
(SERGEY lifts HAROLD and holds a gun to his face) I'm going to kill you.

HAROLD
For free? That doesn't make any sense.

SERGEY
What?

HAROLD
You're a professional. You kill for money. I mean, if you kill me for free, then you'll have to kill a lot of other people to cover your tracks – just throwing away your talent left and right – including killing that SEC agent. And by that time, the FBI will have shut down the airports, and started a dragnet, and all for what? Zero profit. That's what.

NATASHA
Sergey, he's right. This is a setback, but I can make

it up to you. Let us take it from here, and I'll wire you the money as soon as we've settled things.

HAROLD
Look! A freebie! You get paid for not killing. A much better deal.

(Pause)

SERGEY
You are lucky, little man, that I trust Natasha. But I warn you both, if I don't get my money, I will wee wizzit you. *(Beat)*

HAROLD
You'll what?

SERGEY
Wee wizzit you.

HAROLD
One more time.

SERGEY
Wee wizzit! Wee wizzit! I'll come back and wizzit you!

HAROLD
Yes, of course, that's fair. Now, this has been fun, but let me get the door for you. *(Opens the door for SERGEY. SERGEY walks to the door)* It was nice to meet you, Sergey.

(SERGEY gives HAROLD an angry look)

SERGEY
(To NATASHA) Good luck. *(SERGEY exits. Door slam)*

LOUIE
(Poking his head in) Is he gone?

HAROLD
Yes.

LOUIE
Well, lucky him, 'cause I was about to give him...
a decent-sized piece of my mind.

HAROLD
Hey, Louie?

LOUIE
Yes?

HAROLD
FYI? When Sergey had me by the throat? That would've been a good time to stand up for yourself.

LOUIE
I didn't think it would –

HAROLD
Sit down.

LOUIE
OK.

(Meanwhile, GRAMPS has wandered back into the room, with MR. WINKLES)

NATASHA
Now what do we do?

LOUIE
(Heading to the phone) We'll just call an ambulance.

NATASHA
Why?

LOUIE
For Dick Wellington. The rug should keep him

plenty warm till it gets here. *(Picking up the receiver)*

NATASHA
No! *(She hangs up the phone)*

MR. WINKLES
What in the Sam Hill is going on around here?

HAROLD
How long have you been there?

GRAMPS
How long was my last bender? *(Heads to the bar)* I'll have you know I haven't had a drink for over two hours, thank you very much. *(He takes a drink as MR. WINKLES spits out water and makes glubbing noises)*

HAROLD
You've been waiting all day to do that, haven't you?

GRAMPS
Yes!

LOUIE
How does it work? How does it work?

(Enter AGENT SLADEMENGTON, on the phone, so she doesn't notice as NATASHA and HAROLD scoop up the rug from either end, and run upstage and toss it behind the couch, out of sight)

AGENT VIRGINIA SLADEMENGTON
(Carrying a box of paperwork) Yes. Yes. That's what I said. I know. Just have the F.B.I. standing by for the arrest. *(She hangs up. NATASHA*

and HAROLD *have plopped onto the couch in very innocent positions)* Mr. Vanderdoff, who is Advisor X?

HAROLD
Shabbida what?

AGENT VIRGINIA SLADEMENGTON
We talked to your landlord. A charming man. He was more than happy to unlock the office for us, and I had the paperwork brought here. Very interesting stuff. Are you Advisor X?

HAROLD
(We see the spirit drain from him) Alright, that's it. I can't take it anymore. I give up. I'm going to tell you the whole truth.

LOUIE
But Uncle Harold...

HAROLD
Louie, I have to. It's the only way. The truth is...

(Beat)

LOUIE
He merely works for Advisor X. He's one of many feeders that invest in the split-strike conversion plan. *(HAROLD's jaw drops)* Advisor X is the real brains behind Vanderdoff Investments. Harold just brings in clients.

AGENT VIRGINIA SLADEMENGTON
Well, it hasn't taken me long, looking at these numbers, to determine that Advisor X is merely running a large Ponzi scheme.

HAROLD
Louie, No!

LOUIE
Impossible.

NATASHA
I don't even know what a Ponzi scheme is.

LOUIE
(Can only think to say what he should feel) Disbelief!

AGENT VIRGINIA SLADEMENGTON
I am going to need the name of this Advisor X.

LOUIE
I think Harold needs to talk to his lawyer.

AGENT VIRGINIA SLADEMENGTON
(To HAROLD) You're definitely going to need a lawyer if you don't tell me his name.

LOUIE
Uncle Harold, just give your lawyer a call.

AGENT VIRGINIA SLADEMENGTON
Fine. That is your right.

LOUIE
(Looks at AGENT SLADEMENGTON) A little privacy, please?

AGENT VIRGINIA SLADEMENGTON
Very well, I'll give you five minutes. Then you need to tell me everything. (AGENT SLADEMENGTON exits out the front door)

HAROLD
(Hangs up phone) What was that about?

LOUIE
I'm trying to show some initiative. Uncle Harold, you need to think about all those investors! If you get arrested now, we'll never be able to get

their money back to them. It will be confiscated as evidence indefinitely! You need to have faith in the Donnerby investment. When that comes through, we can pay everyone back, and it will be like there never was a Ponzi scheme!

NATASHA
It seems to me, all we need is an Adwisor X.

HAROLD
Well, yes, that would be handy. But where do we find him?

LOUIE
What happened to Dick Wellington?

HAROLD
(to NATASHA) It'd have to be someone the S.E.C. is already gunning for...

LOUIE
Hey, where'd Dick Wellington go?

HAROLD
We put him behind the couch.

NATASHA
(To HAROLD) Someone already perceived as an ewil rich man...

LOUIE
You put Dick Wellington behind the couch? Why?

NATASHA
It's warmer back there! *(Back to HAROLD)* A well connected capitalistic, socio-pathological....

LOUIE
We'll take care of you soon, Dick Wellington.

NATASHA
I've got it! I can say Adwisor X was Dick Wellington!

LOUIE
(Gasps!) Unexpected!

NATASHA
And I can plant enough ewidence to make a conwincing claim.

HAROLD
That sounds good.

NATASHA
I can do it wery easily, no problem. And we can say that is why he disappeared, because he knew he would be exposed.

HAROLD
Wait, wait...

LOUIE
Disappeared? Why, he's right there behind the couch.

NATASHA
Listen Louie, wery shortly my husband will be dead.

LOUIE
Oh, no! Did we not keep him warm enough?

HAROLD
Natasha, I can't let you do that.

NATASHA
You don't have a choice.

HAROLD
Yes, I do. He's a terrible man, but I won't be a

party to it.

LOUIE
What are you talking about? This is no time for a party! We need to think! Hold on! There's still a chance we can get out of this. But not if that agent out there finds out you're Advisor X. If she finds out you're the real Advisor X, then we all go to jail!

GRAMPS
Hey Guys?

HAROLD
(Annoyed) What?

GRAMPS
I'm wearing my hearing aids. *(Beat. This sinks in)* I think I might have a very interesting story to tell my sweet Virginia.

NATASHA
You wouldn't dare!

(NATASHA grabs the frying pan and goes for GRAMPS, but LOUIE throws himself in the way)

LOUIE
No! Don't, please!

NATASHA
Louie, sit down!

LOUIE
Oka– NO! I won't! He's my grampa.

NATASHA
So now you stand up for yourself?

LOUIE
I stand up for family!

GRAMPS
Good boy. *(To HAROLD)* When family is in trouble, we circle the wagons.

HAROLD
What?

GRAMPS
Family pow wow time. *(To NATASHA)* Sorry, lady, just the fellas. *(They huddle up while NATASHA watches suspiciously from a distance)* How 'bout I turn myself in as Advisor X?

HAROLD
Dad, no!

GRAMPS
Listen! By the time your Donnerby thing pays off, they'll realize their mistake and I'll be cleared.

HAROLD
Too risky, what if it doesn't pay off?

GRAMPS
Life is risk, son. Besides, it's always been on my bucket list to spend a night in jail.

HAROLD
No, I'll turn myself in first!

GRAMPS
I don't know. I like the turn me in plan.

HAROLD
Never!

GRAMPS
Fine. So when do you know if this Donnerby thing hits?

HAROLD
(Looking at his watch) Little less than half an hour.

NATASHA
What are you boys talking about ower there?

LOUIE
You know, guy stuff.

GRAMPS
So we just have to keep sweet Virginia distracted for a while.

HAROLD
Sweet Virginia?

GRAMPS
I really like the lady. And now it's time for me to call upon the only power I have.

LOUIE
What power?

GRAMPS
The power of... VENTRILOQUISM. *(He places matching hats on himself and Mr. Winkles. Action hero delivery)* Let's do this.

LOUIE
I'll go get Agent Saladdressingman! *(Runs to the door)*

GRAMPS
And Harold?

HAROLD
Yes?

GRAMPS
You will be doing the human ventriloquist routine.

HAROLD
Wait, no, I –

(AGENT VIRGINIA SLADEMENGTON enters the room)

AGENT VIRGINIA SLADEMENGTON
I will not be diverted! I need to know the truth about Advisor X, I – *(Notices GRAMPS)* Land-a-goshen! What's all this then?

GRAMPS
M'lady, surely you have time for... VENTRILOQUISM.

AGENT VIRGINIA SLADEMENGTON
Well, I don't, but...

GRAMPS
I have saved the best seat for you!

AGENT VIRGINIA SLADEMENGTON
(Melting then clapping her hands together) Okay, just a little time, maybe five minutes.

GRAMPS
We'd like to do a little routine that will tell you everything you'd ever wanna know about Vanderdoff Investments and Advisor X.

HAROLD
(Sotto voce) What are you doing?

GRAMPS
(Sotto voce) Trust me son, this'll be fun. *(To AGENT VIRGINIA SLADEMENGTON)* Just sit right here. *(He places a low stool for her. To LOUIE and NATASHA, pointing to the floor)* You too. Louie! Intro!

(While LOUIE speaks, GRAMPS sets down MR. WINKLES and attaches the mouth piece to HAROLD and holds the cord which allows him to make the mouth open and close)

LOUIE
Ladies and Gentlemen, I have been waiting a long time for this, the human ventriloquist routine starring my grandpa and Uncle Harold. Everyone put your hands together in the clapping sort of way for the two greatest guys in the history of forever!

(AGENT VIRGINIA SLADEMENGTON and LOUIE clap enthusiastically. All sit with their backs' to the audience to watch GRAMPS)

GRAMPS
Okay, we just have to get this hooked up here, there we are. How does it feel?

(For the rest of the routine, when it's indicated that DUMMY HAROLD is speaking, it is, in fact, GRAMPS speaking for HAROLD, as he makes the mouth move)

DUMMY HAROLD
It feels just fine, please and thank you very much!

(LOUIE finds the voice very amusing)

LOUIE
Classic! Classic.

GRAMPS
Say, Harold, I heard you ran into Cinderella today?

DUMMY HAROLD
Yeah, she was sad her photos hadn't arrived on time.

GRAMPS
Oh, what'd she say?

DUMMY HAROLD
(Singing) Some day, my prints will come.

LOUIE
Boom goes the dynamite! That's funny cause it's true.

AGENT VIRGINIA SLADEMENGTON
Oh dear. *(Laughing)* Oh dear.

GRAMPS
I heard you tried to make a three level cake today, how'd that go?

DUMMY HAROLD
Oh, it all ended in tiers. Three of them. So: Success!

LOUIE
OH! I see what you did there.

AGENT VIRGINIA SLADEMENGTON
Ha! Hahaha! My stomach hurts. Stop.

HAROLD
So dad, on the way here, I met a toad.

GRAMPS
A toad, you say?

DUMMY HAROLD
I asked him why toads never sit on toadstools.

GRAMPS
What'd he say?

DUMMY HAROLD
Because there isn't mushroom.

LOUIE
Oh man, I don't need to hear another joke ever.

AGENT VIRGINIA SLADEMENGTON
You are a caution. But I have to say, as much fun as this is, I need to find out about Advisor X-

GRAMPS
(Similtaneously) Advisor X, exactly. I knew you wouldn't let us tell jokes forever. Smart and beautiful. I believe we promised sweet Virginia here that we'd get to the bottom of this.

DUMMY HAROLD
But wait, Dad?

GRAMPS
Yes?

DUMMY HAROLD
Before we do that, I just want to say something.

GRAMPS
Go ahead, son.

DUMMY HAROLD
I love you dad. I know I don't say it enough, but, I love you.

GRAMPS
I love you too, son. And I'm proud of you.

(GRAMPS hugs HAROLD)

LOUIE
Aww. That's nice.

GRAMPS
You know I raised you right, son. To believe in family. Family comes first.

DUMMY HAROLD
I know Dad.

(NATASHA notices the Panzadrine)

GRAMPS
You have to be willing to sacrifice everything for family, son.

(NATASHA, with her back to the show, fills the syringe in front of the audience)

GRAMPS
Sometimes, when people make sacrifices, they need to go away for a bit.

DUMMY HAROLD
But I never worry, because I know they'll be back.

GRAMPS
That's right. Sweet Virginia, I have to confess, Advisor X is in this very room.

HAROLD
(Taking off the mask) Dad, no –

GRAMPS
Be quiet, Harold! This is my confession. It's time the truth comes out.

HAROLD
Dad, I won't let you!

GRAMPS
Advisor X, is, in fact *(holding up his hands to be cuffed)* –

(At this moment, NATASHA manages to plunge the syringe into GRAMPS' butt, without letting AGENT SLADEMENGTON and LOUIE see anything, but HAROLD has seen it all. GRAMPS freezes in place. NATASHA starts to applaud, enthusiastically. LOUIE, a bit confused, joins in)

AGENT VIRGINIA SLADEMENGTON
(Leaping to his feet and running to GRAMPS)
Oh, dear Lord! What's wrong with him?

HAROLD
(As if suddenly noticing that GRAMPS is frozen)
Oh, dear, he's had one of his fits.

AGENT VIRGINIA SLADEMENGTON
Fits?

HAROLD
Yes, he's recently developed a rare version of narcolepsy. He just freezes right up.

LOUIE
I didn't know that.

HAROLD
Well, you should come around more often! Louie, help me get him to his bedroom.

AGENT VIRGINIA SLADEMENGTON
I'll do it. Look out now.

(AGENT VIRGINIA SLADEMENGTON and LOUIE grab GRAMPS and start to carry him offstage)

AGENT VIRGINIA SLADEMENGTON
Oh Lord, don't you take this man from me, I want to get to know him.

(AGENT SLADEMENGTON and LOUIE get GRAMPS offstage)

HAROLD
(To NATASHA) You shot him up with that Panzadrine stuff?!

NATASHA
I thought he was going to spill the beans!

HAROLD
He was trying to take the fall, not that I would have let him, but you didn't have to paralyze him! He put his hands up like this! That's the universal "cuff me" gesture!

NATASHA
I thought he wanted a double fist bump!

HAROLD
Are you sure that panzadrine stuff is safe?

NATASHA
Perfectly.

HAROLD
Alright. Okay. 15 minutes till Donnerby hits. It's up to us to stall.

NATASHA
What?...

HAROLD
Stall!

AGENT VIRGINIA SLADEMENGTON
(Entering) He's utterly frozen! Is he going to be alright?

HAROLD
Oh, my poor father. It's so sad, seeing age take

its toll. You never want to see your parents in decline, but it is inevitable. It's all part of the circle of life. That connects us all.

AGENT VIRGINIA SLADEMENGTON
Oh no! Should we call an ambulance?

HAROLD
No, no. He always snaps right out of it. It's just- *(Starting to fight back tears)* It is so unfair, what happens when you get older. *(LOUIE enters)* Oh, Louie, you have to promise me, when I start to lose my mental acuity *(Becoming emotional)*, you have to just pull the plug.

LOUIE
(It's a given) No problem.

HAROLD
You can't let emotion get in the way. You have to put aside – *(Realization take to LOUIE)* – No problem?

LOUIE
I will pull that plug.

HAROLD
Just like that, huh? You will pull that plug? Just send me to the great beyond without a second thought?

LOUIE
No, that's not –

HAROLD
You ungrateful little monster! *(Going to the bar and grabbing a lemon zester)* Here! Here's the easy grip lemon zester! Take it and stab me in the heart. The heart that thought you loved me! O, foolish heart!

LOUIE
Uncle Harold, I love you so much!

HAROLD
You shut your betrayal hole! Do you even remember the exact moment you lost your humanity?

AGENT VIRGINIA SLADEMENGTON
Mr. Vanderdoff! I need some answers.

HAROLD
Don't we all? Why? Why?! Why do the people you love the most, always hurt you the worst?! WHY?!

AGENT VIRGINIA SLADEMENGTON
(Fighting to get control of the room) Mr. Vanderdoff, pull yourself together!

(AGENT SLADEMENGTON throws a glass of water in HAROLD's face. This helps calm HAROLD down)

HAROLD
Okay. Okay, okay.

AGENT VIRGINIA SLADEMENGTON
I think we owe it to your father to find out what triggered his attack. He was just saying that Advisor X was in this very room. Now, I know I'm not Advisor X. *(To LOUIE)* Are you Advisor X?

HAROLD
No, he's not!

AGENT VIRGINIA SLADEMENGTON
(To NATASHA) Are you Advisor X?

HAROLD
Of course she's not!

AGENT VIRGINIA SLADEMENGTON
Ah-Ha! Just as I suspected all along. *(Looking to HAROLD)* That means Advisor X has got to be –

(AGENT SLADEMENGTON is cut off by a loud groan from behind the couch. DICK WELLINGTON appears, untangling himself from the rug)

NATASHA
(The first to emerge from this new shock, tries this on for size) Oh…Dickie, darling…are you feeling better?

DICK WELLINGTON
What the hell happened?

HAROLD
You had your big idea, then some drinks, then you needed to lay down.

LOUIE
I think you mean lie down.

DICK WELLINGTON
What?

LOUIE
One lays down an object, but people lie down.

AGENT VIRGINIA SLADEMENGTON
You mean he's not a wax figure?

HAROLD
No, no. You were completely right. He was a wax figure, but because he so wanted to be a real boy *(beat)* he was granted the gift of life. It's a regular holiday miracle. Of course it's Dick Wellington!

AGENT VIRGINIA SLADEMENGTON
Mr. Wellington, are you Advisor X? *(Pause)* What

do you have to say for yourself?

DICK WELLINGTON
I don't remember anything.

AGENT VIRGINIA SLADEMENGTON
What do you mean you don't remember anything?

DICK WELLINGTON
I can't even remember my own name. Who are you idiots?

AGENT VIRGINIA SLADEMENGTON
Mr. Wellington, I'm Agent Slademengton of the Securities and Exchange Commission. You have sleazed your way out of seventeen different convictions on my watch with petty technicalities and witness tampering. Now I'm asking you: are you Advisor X?

DICK WELLINGTON
Who is this cow, and why isn't she out to pasture?

AGENT VIRGINIA SLADEMENGTON
Looks like we've found Advisor X.

(Beat. Then, the next three lines are nearly simultaneous as they point at DICK)

LOUIE
Yep, it was him alright!

NATASHA
No doubt about it.

HAROLD
Here's your Advisor X.

NATASHA
Heartbreaking as it is to me, I can prowide you proof that my husband created this Ponzi scheme

and duped poor Harold here.

AGENT VIRGINIA SLADEMENGTON
Dick Wellington, as an agent of the Securities and Exchange Commission, I am placing you under arrest. You need to come with me to headquarters.

DICK WELLINGTON
What?

NATASHA
Don't worry darling, I'll be with you ewery step of the way. *(With a look to HAROLD)* To make sure things go smoothly.

AGENT VIRGINIA SLADEMENGTON
Well, Mr. Vanderdoff, looks like you're off the hook for now, but I have a list of every one of your clients. If you make sure that no client loses a single penny, the S.E.C. is willing to turn a blind eye to a reformed investor. We have bigger fish to fry. Besides, I'd hate to see you sharing a cell with Mr. Wellington here.

DICK WELLINGTON
I don't like sharing. That much I remember.

AGENT VIRGINIA SLADEMENGTON
I shall bid you good day sir. *(Handing HAROLD a piece of paper)* And...have your father call me.

HAROLD
Will do.

AGENT VIRGINIA SLADEMENGTON
(She reacts in sexual anticipation) Come on now, Mr. Wellington. *(Exit AGENT SLADEMENGTON and DICK)*

NATASHA
(Giving HAROLD a double fist bump) Wictory! *(NATASHA exits)*

HAROLD
What time is it?

LOUIE
Three o'clock.

HAROLD
Donnerby! *(He rushes to turn the TV on. We hear a news anchor. Background sounds of a marching band)*

ANCHOR
(From the TV, the broadcast already in progress) – news hour. At the Ham Parade earlier today, hundreds of people were delighted by the sight of free hams being tossed –

(HAROLD changes the channel. We hear a horse race in progress. HAROLD and LOUIE's conversation overlaps the horse race)

ANNOUNCER
– and heading into the final turn, Mother's Hat Box is in the lead, EZPay continues to chase her in earnest, followed by Donnerby, right along side Inside Information. By the Numbers is five off the lead, center of the track is Pants on Fire, fourth to the outside comes TooBigToFail and MyWifeKnowsEverything is dead last. Look out, Donnerby is moving up, Mother's Hat Box still in the lead by a length and a half. It's Rubberband in the stretch, and Cabbage by a head. Who knew? And here comes TooBigToFail, Mother's Hat Box falling back, no

chance for MyWifeKnowsEverything, into the final furlong, it's Donnerby and TooBigToFail, neck and neck, there they go folks. Donnerby at 20 to 1 is putting on a good show today.

LOUIE
Donnerby is a horse?

HAROLD
Yes.

LOUIE
That was the investment?

HAROLD
Yes

LOUIE
Shut the front door! You put 900,000 on a horse?

HAROLD
Shhh! Watch!

LOUIE
ARE YOU KIDDING ME?! YOU PUT IT ALL ON A HORSE?!

HAROLD
COME ON DONNERBY!

LOUIE
I'm gonna give you such a pinch! *(He does)*

HAROLD
OW! That really hurt!

LOUIE
Look, there he goes! COME ON DONNERBY!

ANNOUNCER
TooBigToFail stumbles and it's all Donnerby!

(HAROLD and LOUIE scream like little girls and jump up and down with glee) Inside Information second, and By the Numbers third.

(LOUIE runs over to the stereo and turns the music back on. Time to celebrate. They dance. Front door opens. JUDITH enters. She takes in the carnage. She walks over and turns off the TV and music)

JUDITH
I just spoke with an Agent Slademengton outside. She told me everything.

HAROLD
Judith!

JUDITH
So Dick Wellington tricked you into helping him run a giant Ponzi scheme?

HAROLD
No.

LOUIE
Yes, but thanks to Harold's genius-

HAROLD
No! No more lies, Judith. I was running a Ponzi scheme.

JUDITH
You?! I had over a half a million dollars of my own money invested with you.

HAROLD
I know!

JUDITH
And all of our friends!

HAROLD
What a fool I've been! I'm sorry.

JUDITH
And now is it gone?

LOUIE
Nope. Thanks to a *(gives HAROLD a playful noogie)* wise investment of our own, everyone gets back their investment with the 20% interest! And best of all, Panda Fest is saved! Hurray!

HAROLD
And now, Judith, I swear, it's all over. Vanderdoff Investments will close its doors forever.

LOUIE
And I can devote my full time to being in charge of Panda Fest. And to being in charge in general. I like showing initiative!

JUDITH
But you were lying to me all these years?

HAROLD
Yes, but I did it all for you!

JUDITH
What do you mean?

HAROLD
I thought if I worked hard enough, I could make you happy.

JUDITH
You make me happy. Just you, not your work.

HAROLD
I'm so sorry. I was wrong. I never meant to hurt you.

JUDITH
But you did.

HAROLD
I know. How can I make it up to you?

(Beat)

LOUIE
Well, you know, I believe the Society for the Ethical Treatment of Animals with One Eye is looking for a new co-chair.

HAROLD
Absolutely! *(To JUDITH, on one knee)* Judith, I'll do anything you want. I'm yours from now on.

JUDITH
Well, I could use a partner for all my charity work.

HAROLD
I'll do it.

JUDITH
But you need to honest with me from now on.

HAROLD
Absolutely.

JUDITH
And you're going to have to earn my trust again.

HAROLD
I will. I love you so much, Judith.

JUDITH
Oh, Harold, I've missed you. *(They kiss)*

LOUIE
Well, that settles it. And of course you'll both sit

on the board of Panda Fest.

HAROLD
Ahhh...?

LOUIE
You will, 'cause I'm large and in charge!

HAROLD
Okay, okay!

LOUIE
(Squeezing the HAROLD and JUDITH together)
Now that's what I like to see! A legitimate happy ending, no muss, no fuss!

(GRAMPS hops in, half-paralyzed, face in frozen expression, holding the seltzer bottle)

GRAMPS
Harold, I can't believe you –

HAROLD
Oh my goodness! Dad! *(He rushes over to hug him)* I'm so sorry. It was Natasha –

(Before HAROLD can finish his sentence, GRAMPS sprays him in the mouth. Music starts and a chase ensues. LOUIE tries to intervene, but gets blasted by the seltzer bottle. HAROLD runs to the front door and opens it, revealing AGENT SLADEMENGTON. She sees what's happening and rushes in to help. She scoops up GRAMPS in her arms, overjoyed that he is somewhat recovered. She kisses him. She carries him around to help him get a better angle for spraying HAROLD and LOUIE. Wild chaos as the curtain falls)

END OF PLAY

ABOUT THE PLAYWRIGHT

Joe Foust is a sexy beast. A writer, actor, director, and fight director based in Chicago, Joe has acted at The Goodman, Steppenwolf, Wisdom Bridge, Remy Bumppo, Next, TheaterWit, Court, Chicago Shakespeare Theatre, First Folio, Penninsula Players, Cleveland Playhouse, Syracuse Stage, New Victory on Broadway, Maltz Jupiter, Milwaukee Shakespeare and is a founding member of Defiant Theater, where his credits include directing and either writing or co-writing ACTION MOVIE: THE PLAY, SCI-FI ACTION MOVIE IN SPACE PRISON, HORROR MOVIE: THE PLAY, and UBU RAW. He is currently penning a Robin Hood play with John Maclay.

As Nick Offerman said about Joe on LATE NIGHT WITH DAVID LETTERMAN, "When I saw him, I said to myself, 'I wanna hang with this guy. He knows just the kind of trouble I want to get into.'"

More Plays From SORDELET INK

It Came From Mars
by Joseph Zettelmaier

Ebeneezer - A Christmas Play
by Joseph Zettelmaier

The Gravedigger - A Frankenstein play
by Joseph Zettelmaier

The Scullery Maid
by Joseph Zettelmaier

Dead Man's Shoes
by Joseph Zettelmaier

A Tale of Two Cities
by Christoper M Walsh
adapted from the novel by Charles Dickens

the Count of Monte Cristo
by Christoper M Walsh
adapted from the novel by Alexandre Dumas

the Moonstone
by Robert Kauzlaric
adapted from the novel by Wilkie Collins

Season on the Line
by Shawn Pfautsch
adapted from Herman Melville's Moby Dick

Eve of Ides
by David Blixt

Visit www.sordeletink.com for more!

NOVELS FROM
SORDELET INK

The Star-Cross'd Series
THE MASTER OF VERONA
VOICE OF THE FALCONER
FORTUNE'S FOOL
THE PRINCE'S DOOM
VARNISH'D FACES & OTHER SHORT STORIES

The Colossus Series
COLOSSUS: STONE & STEEL
COLOSSUS: THE FOUR EMPERORS

and coming 2016
COLOSSUS: WAIL OF THE FALLEN

HER MAJESTY'S WILL
a novel of Wit & Kit

All by bestselling author David Blixt!

And coming in 2016
THE DRAGONTAIL BUTTONHOLE
a novel of WWII Europe
by Peter Curtis

Visit www.sordeletink.com for more!

PRAISE FOR
ONCE A PONZI TIME

"A wild roller coaster of a comedy, with a cast of characters and increasingly hilarious situations that only the incredibly inventive Joe Foust could have created." - *Paul Slade Smith, playwright of UNNECESSARY FARCE*

"Joe Foust's Once a Ponzi Time is an unabashedly silly romp that actually turns the infamous Ponzi scheme into material for big laughs. Watching Ponzi is like getting on a roller coaster that, once it gets to the top, takes you on a breakneck ride, pulls out every stop and almost physically throws you around with each plot twist and turn. If you like fun, wackiness and strong physical comedy, you'll love Once A Ponzi Time!" - *Sean Grennan, playwright of MAKING GOD LAUGH*

"99% of what's called comedy barely makes me grin. Once A Ponzi Time made me laugh out loud." - *Tim Kazurinsky, of SNL fame*

Printed in Poland
by Amazon Fulfillment
Poland Sp. z o.o., Wrocław